Claudio Aboy

Cesar Britez

Michal Dutkiewicz

Gonzalo Flores

Diego Florio

Danilo Guida

Dario Hartmann

Brian LeBlanc

Anibal Maraschi

Perla Perlucky

Marcelo Sosa

Daniel Suarez

Flirt!

The Art of Naughty
Volume Two

"ooh...look at the pretty lady..."
You might have been 8 or 9 years old when your dad let you tag along to pick up the family wagon at the gas station. The heady aroma of fresh oil and burnt tires mixed with the sweat and dirt of a mechanic who looked like he could pull the bumper off a Buick with his bare hands. Oh, this was a MAN'S place, where cherry-red cigar stubs stuck out of unshaven faces and dirty jokes ran thick and heavy like 10W30. And always in the back of such a shop, a trio of carlifts would stand like polished sentinels of masculinity, guarding a temple of pure fantasy - the girlie calendar! That young lady in the illustration holding the oversized wrench, sparkplug, or lugnut was promising more than good mileage and maintenance. Her angelic face with its unselfish smile told you, at your whim, she'd be happy to hold YOUR lugnuts, and lube you up every 3000 miles!

No matter where you saw your first pin-up, in a garage, an advertisement, or your dad's sock drawer, it was your introduction to "woman as goddess" - the ultimate fantasy of female as mother-sister-friend-lover...without all that irksome Oedipal luggage! However, in today's more high-speed, over-caffeinated, 24/7 all-anal-midget porn-driven world, that winsome innocence has been lost. Now any webhead with a digital camera and a loose-limbed girlfriend can get as gyno-centric and labia-riffic as they like. Where's the sport in that? Fascinating to be sure, but just a tad too clinical for our tastes! The pin-up painting offers a little something for the imagination. You DO remember the imagination, don't you? That poor little dried-up gland deep inside your melon that hardly ever gets to come out and play? Well, that's why we created Flirt! This will be an on-going showcase of "The Art of Naughty" that will give some of today's artists a chance to re-imagine the classic pin-up. We hope you enjoy the show, and will come back to sample future volumes. And yeah, get your oil changed!

Sal Quartuccio & Bob Keenan - Publishers

Front cover painting by Michal Dutkiewicz.

Flirt! - The Art of Naughty Volume Two
All artwork is copyright © 2005 their respective artists.
Flirt! Volume Two © 2005 S.Q. Productions Inc. All rights reserved.
Printed in Hong Kong. Book design by Grassy Knoll Studios.

Published by SQP Inc. - PO Box 248 - Columbus, NJ 08022
Always on the web at www.sqpinc.com

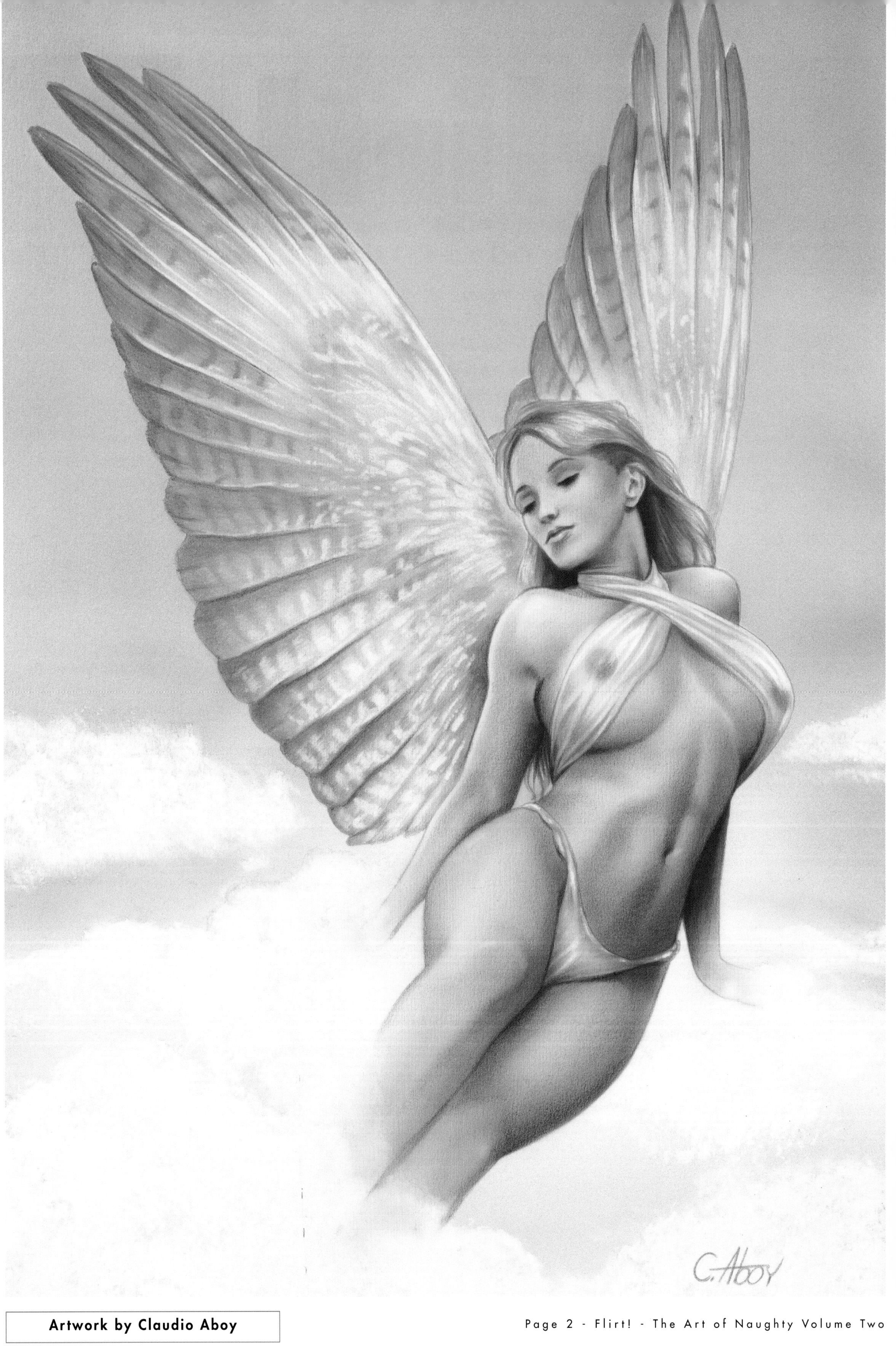
C.Aboy

Artwork by Claudio Aboy

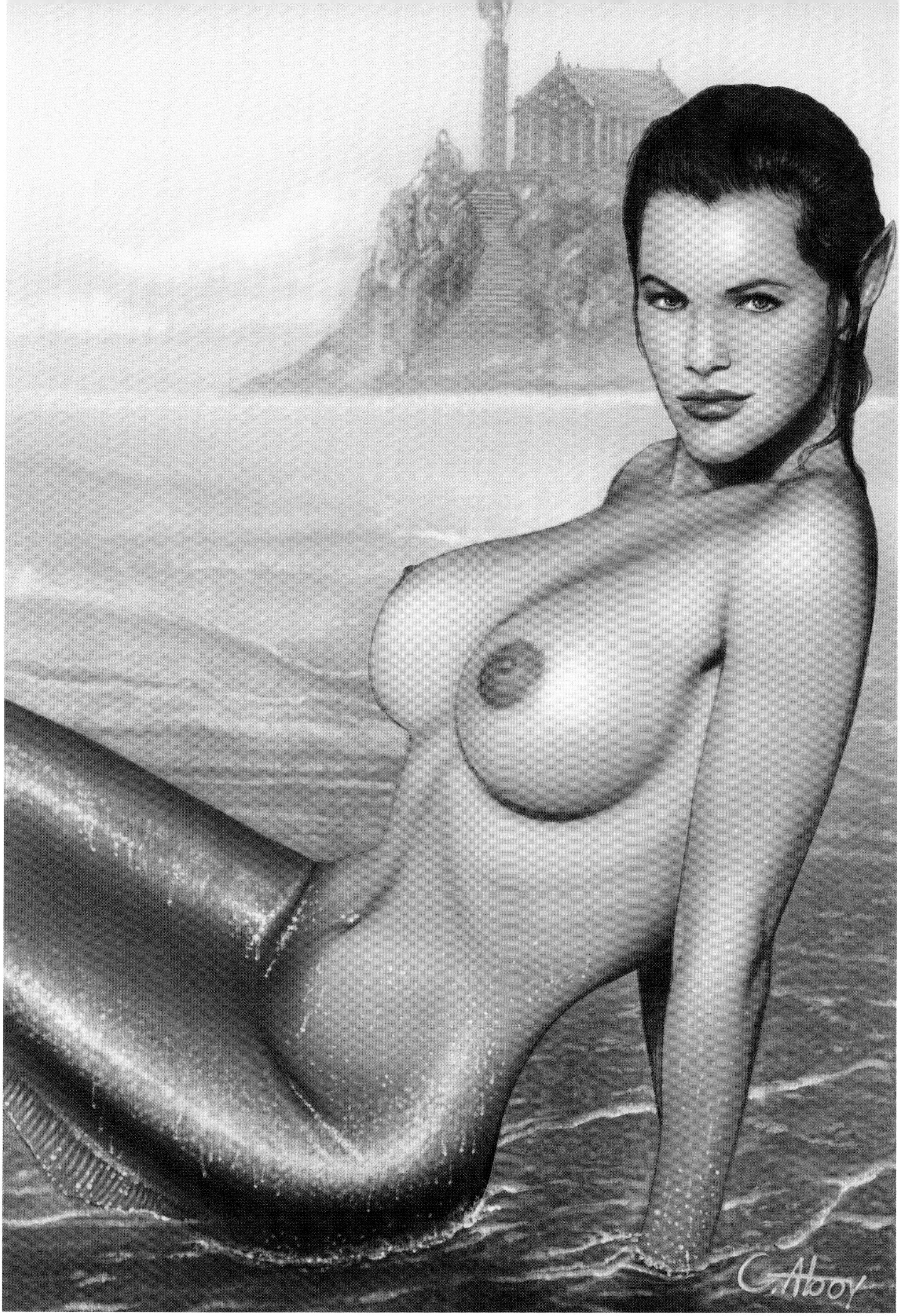
C. Aboy

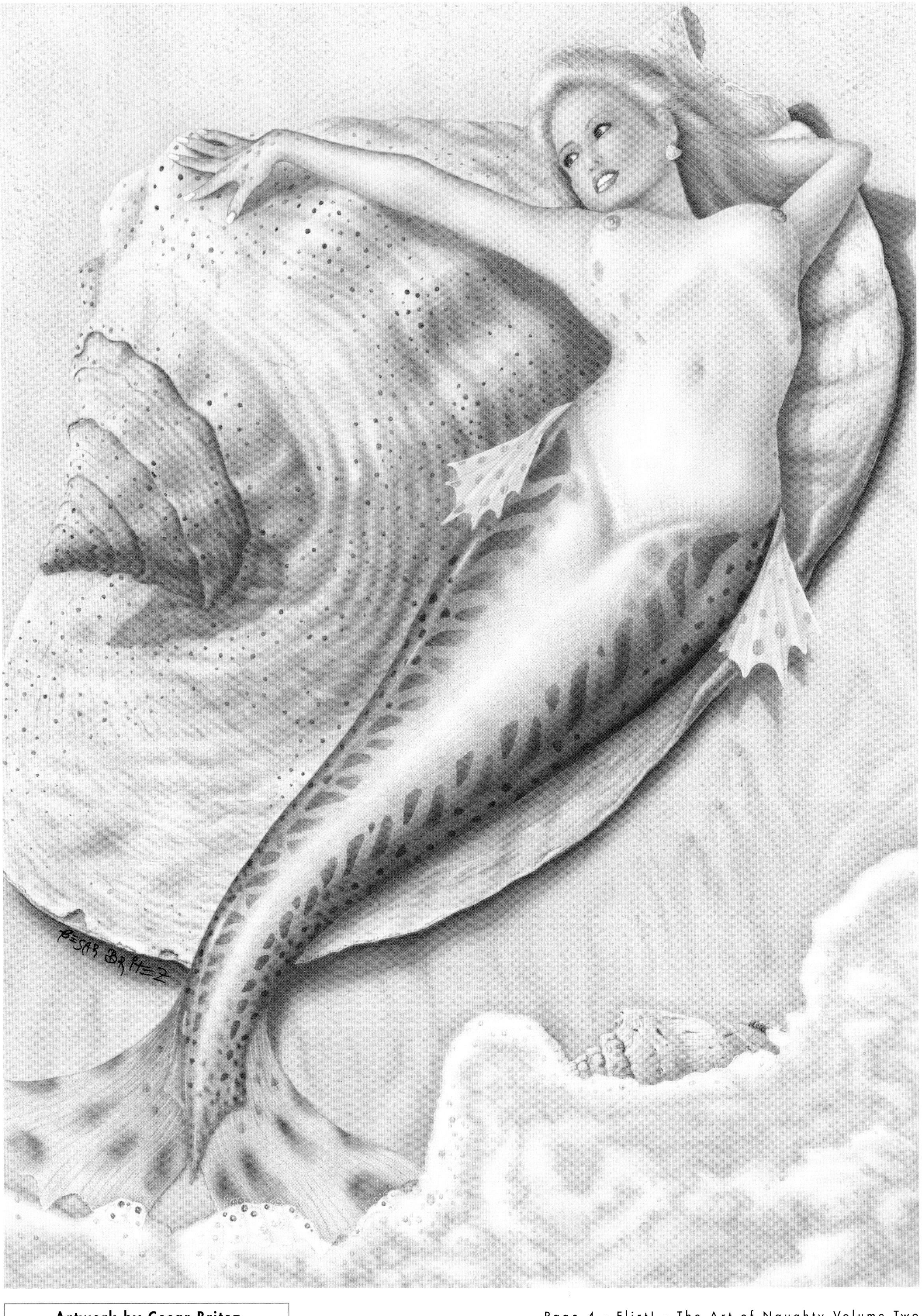

Artwork by Cesar Britez

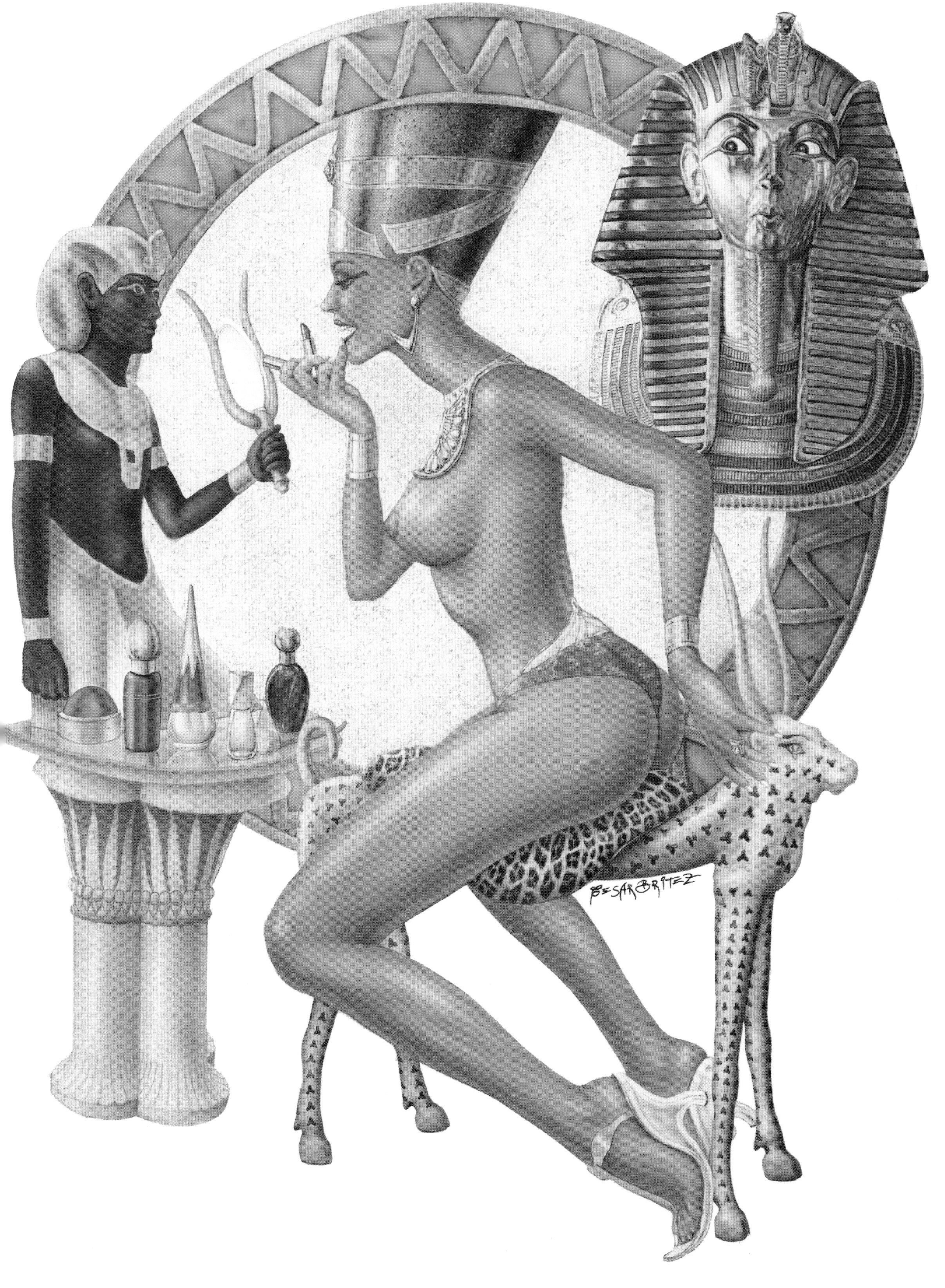
CESAR BRITEZ

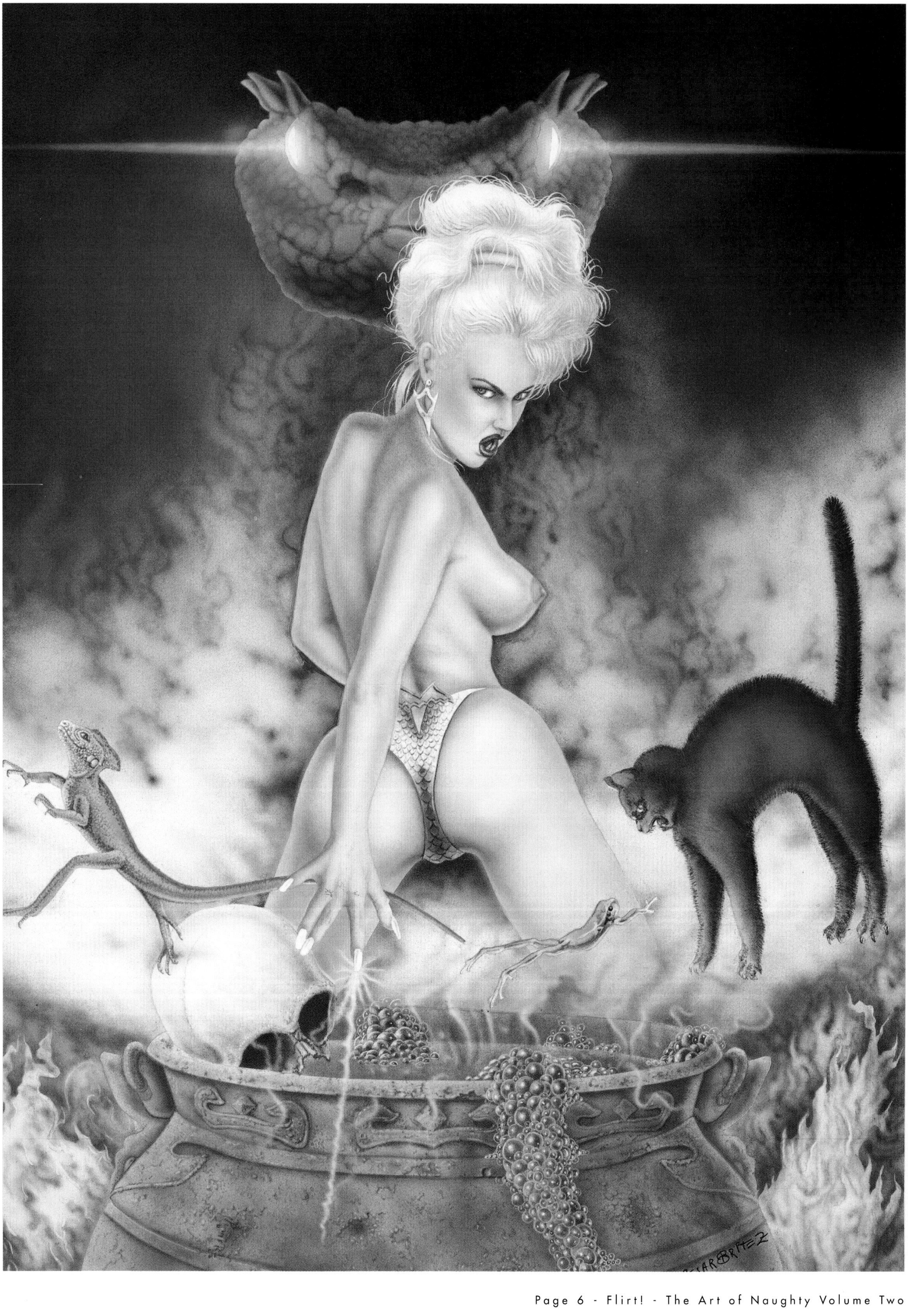

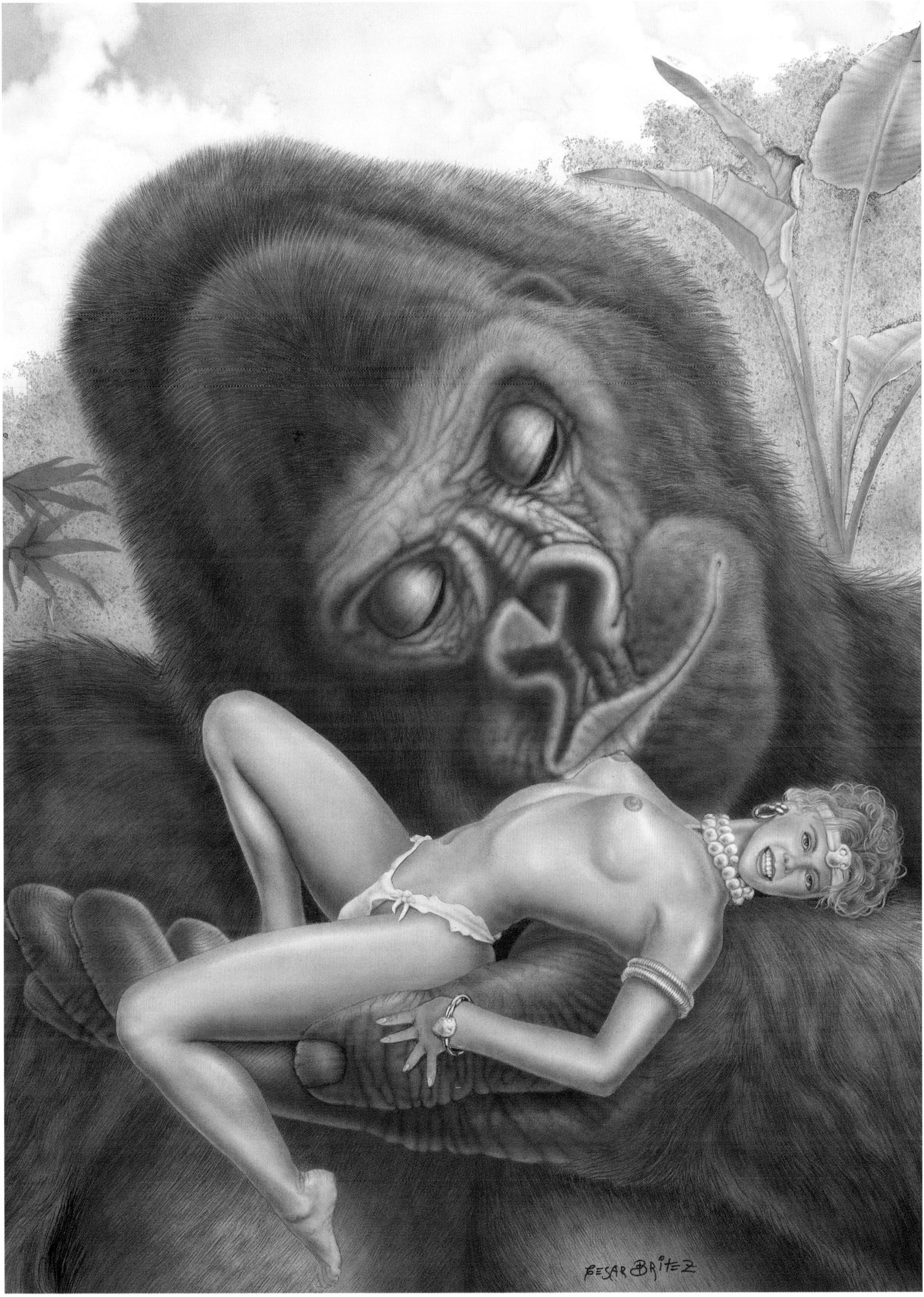

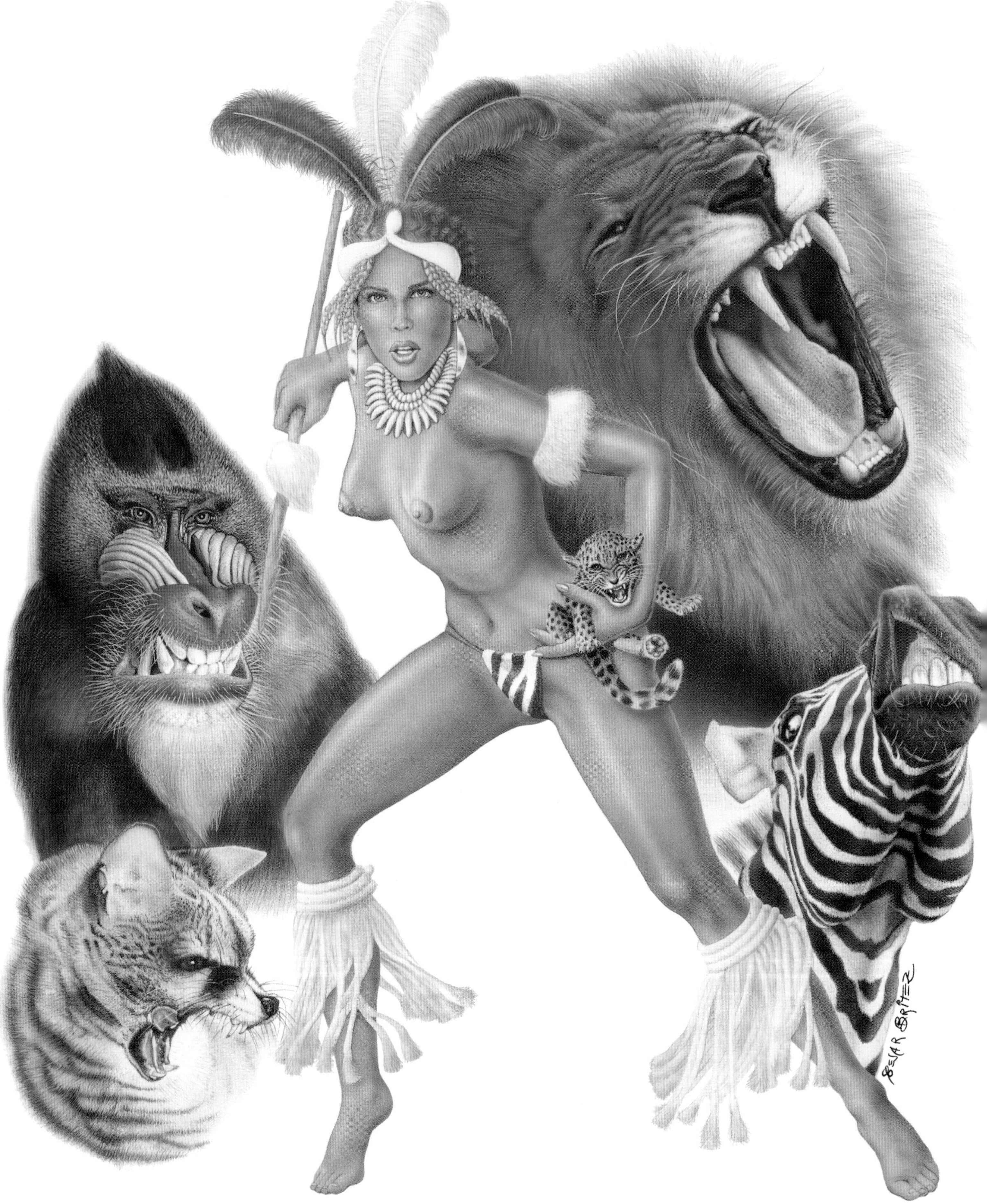

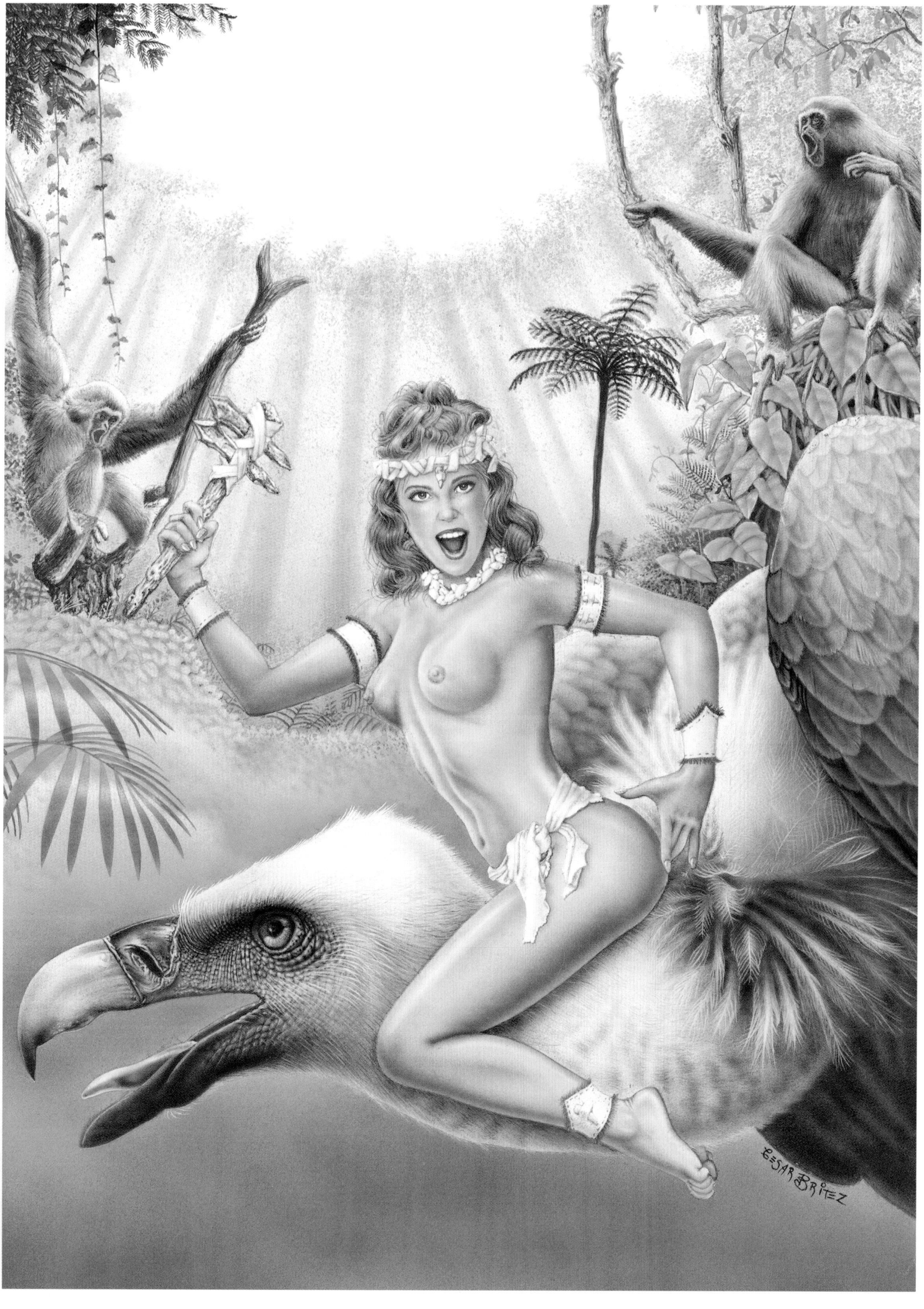
CESAR BRITEZ

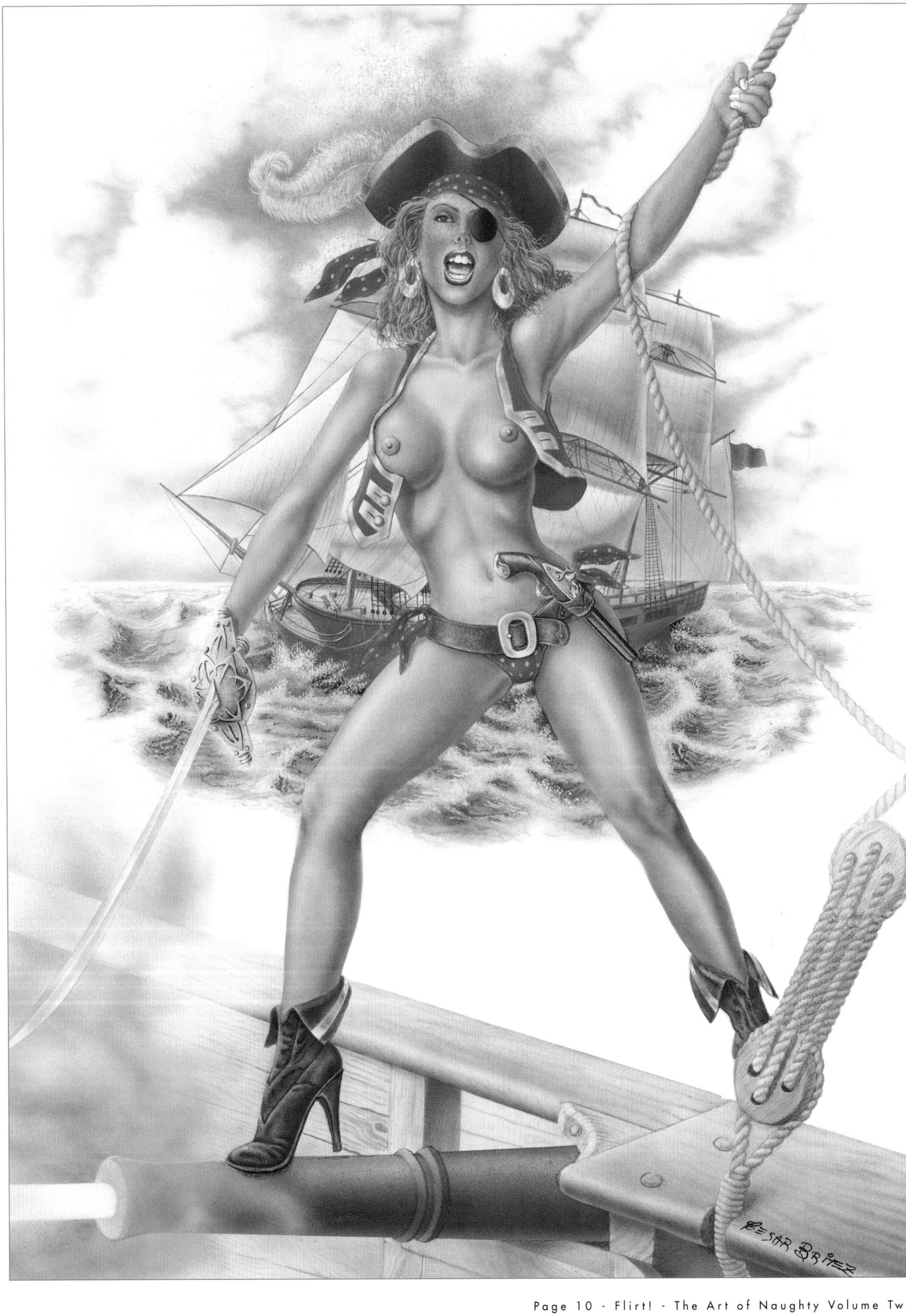

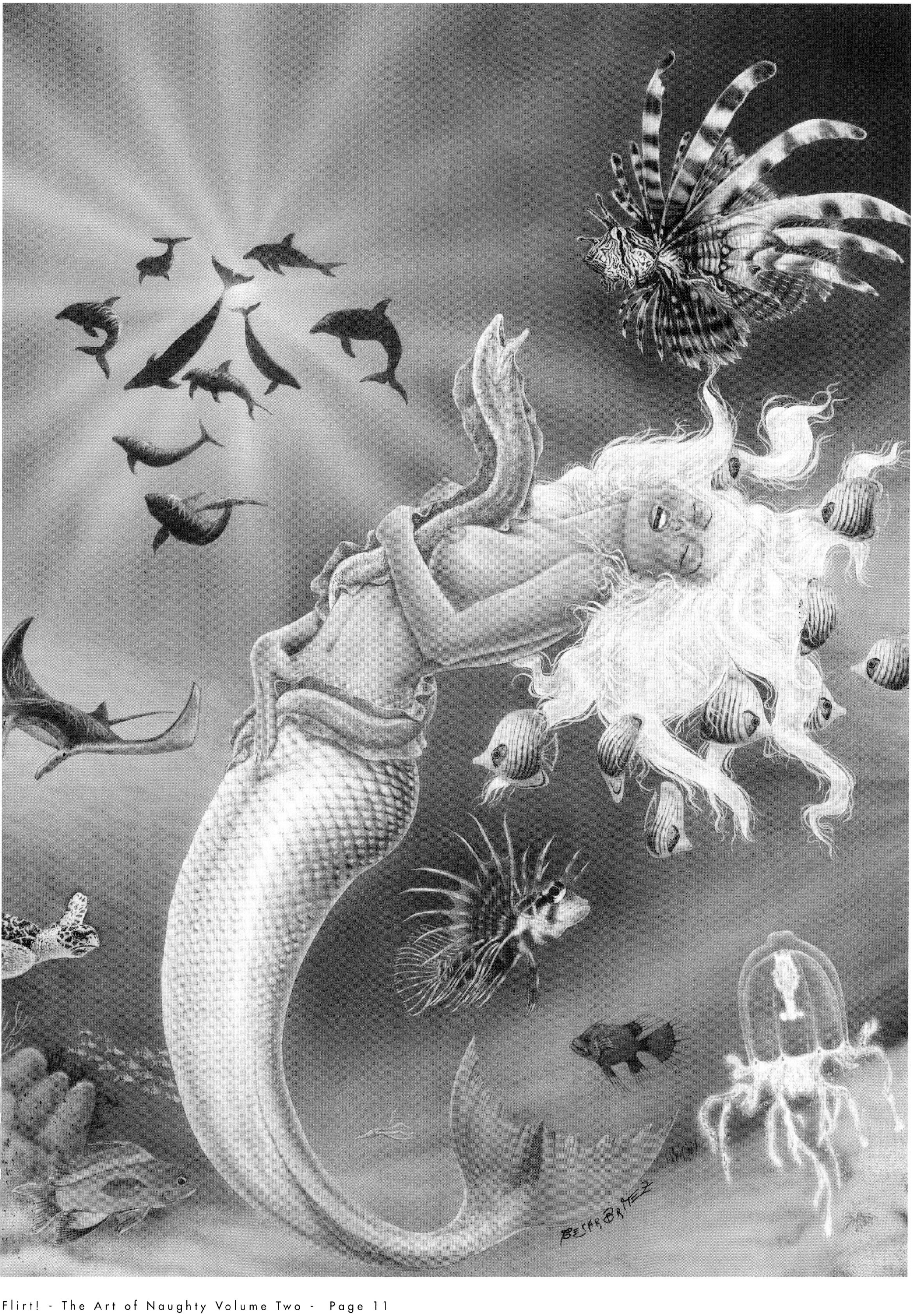
CESAR BRITEZ

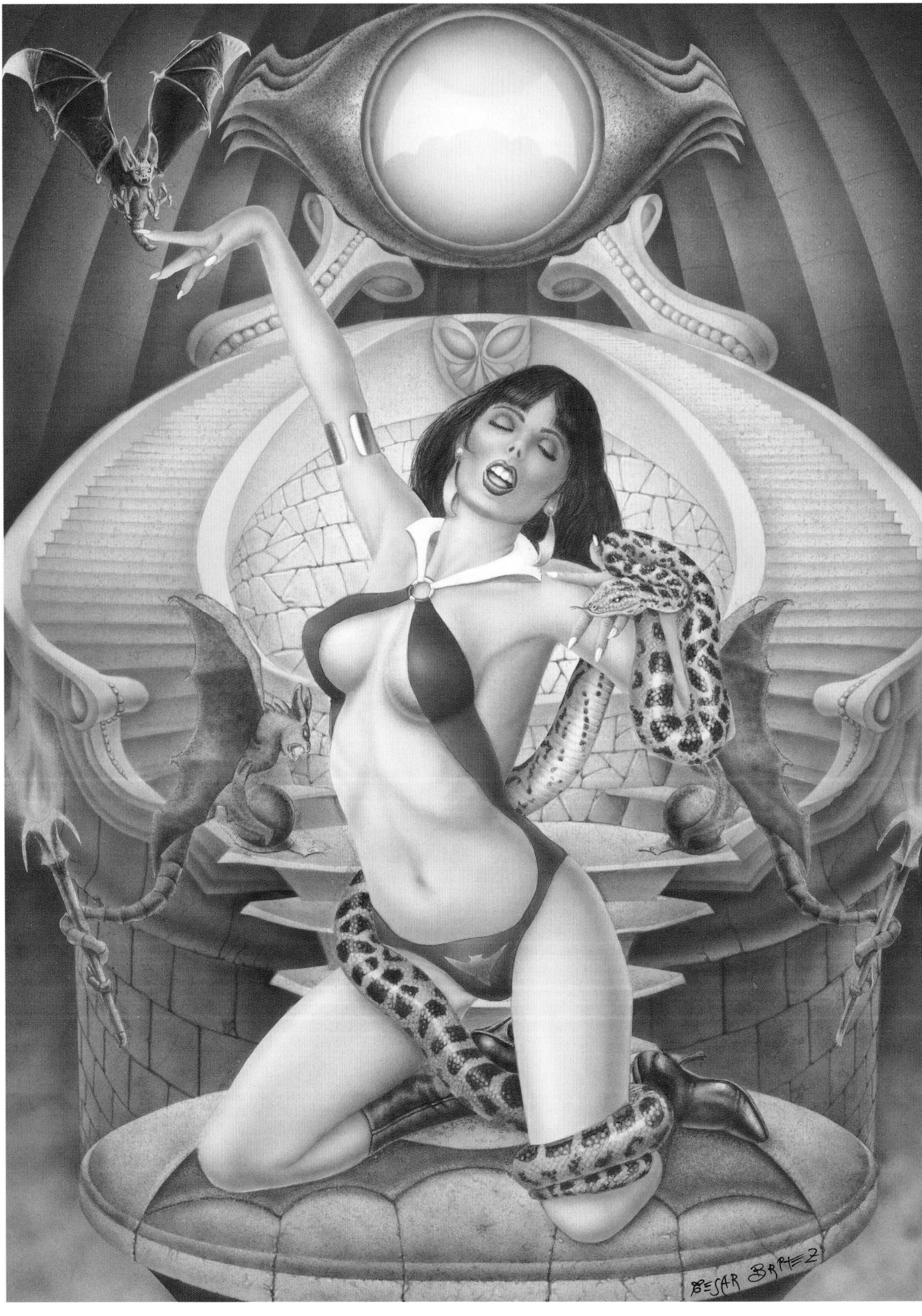

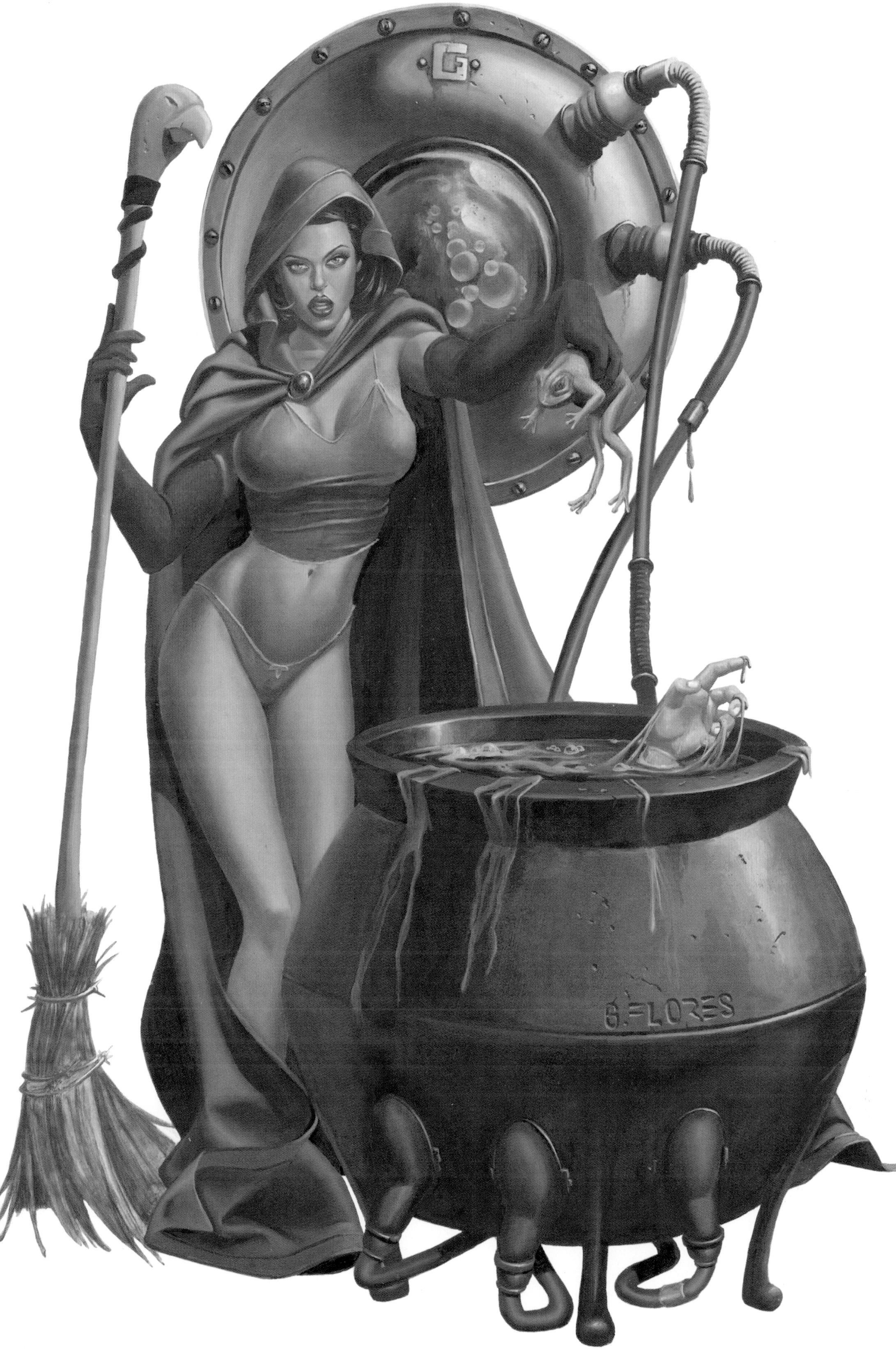
G
G.FLORES

Artwork by Gonzalo Flores

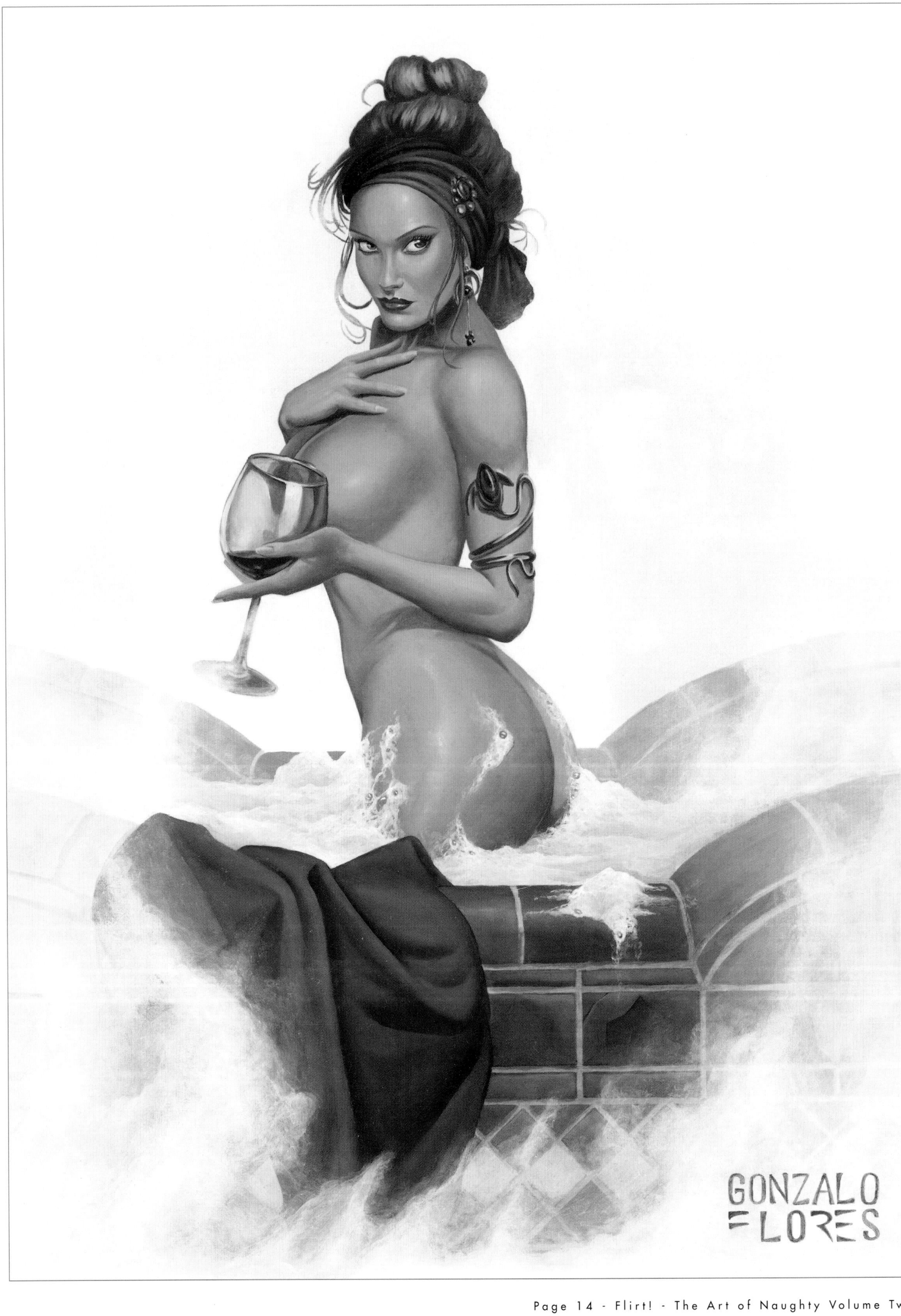
GONZALO
FLORES

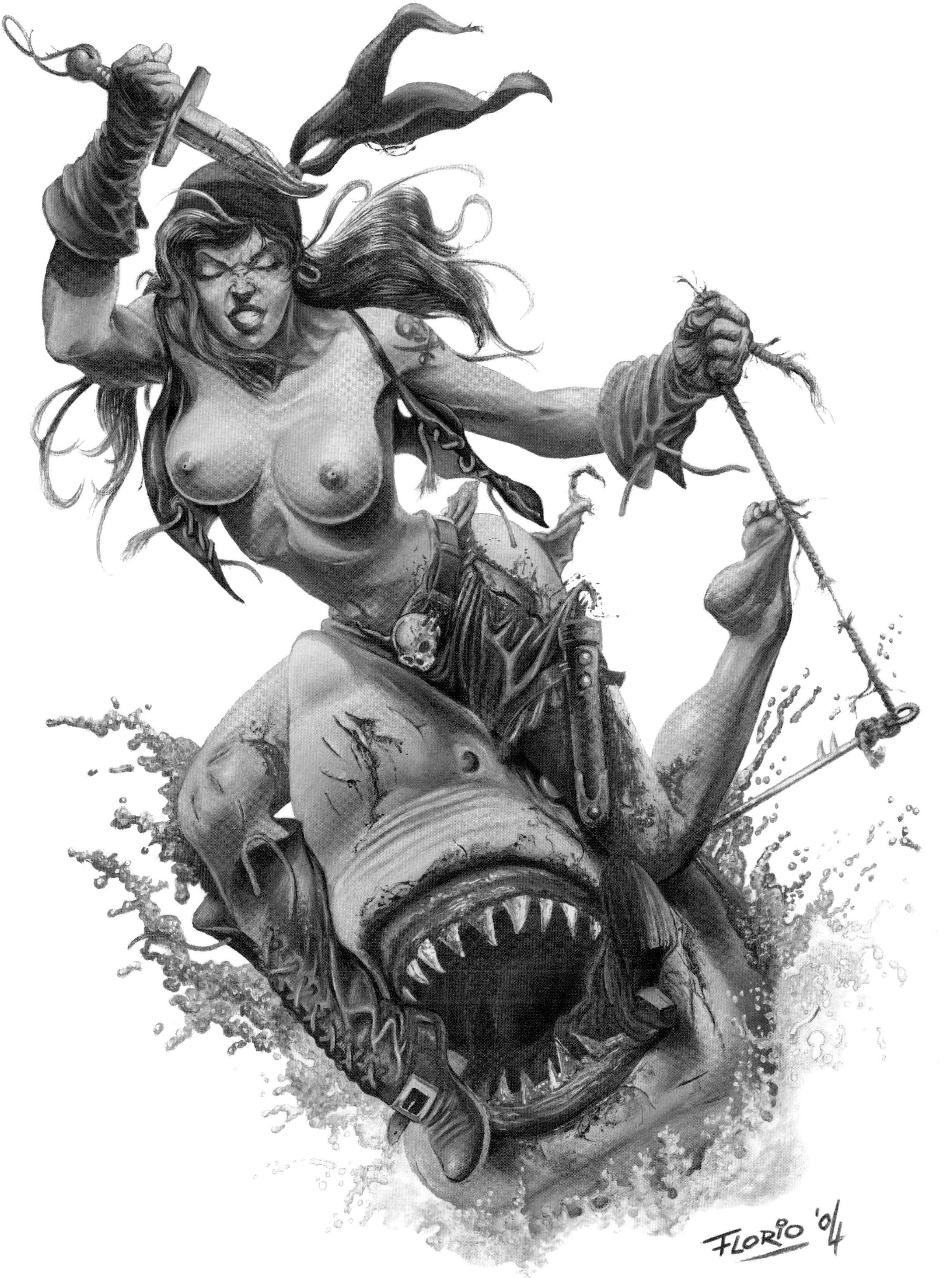
FLORIO '04

Artwork by Diego Florio

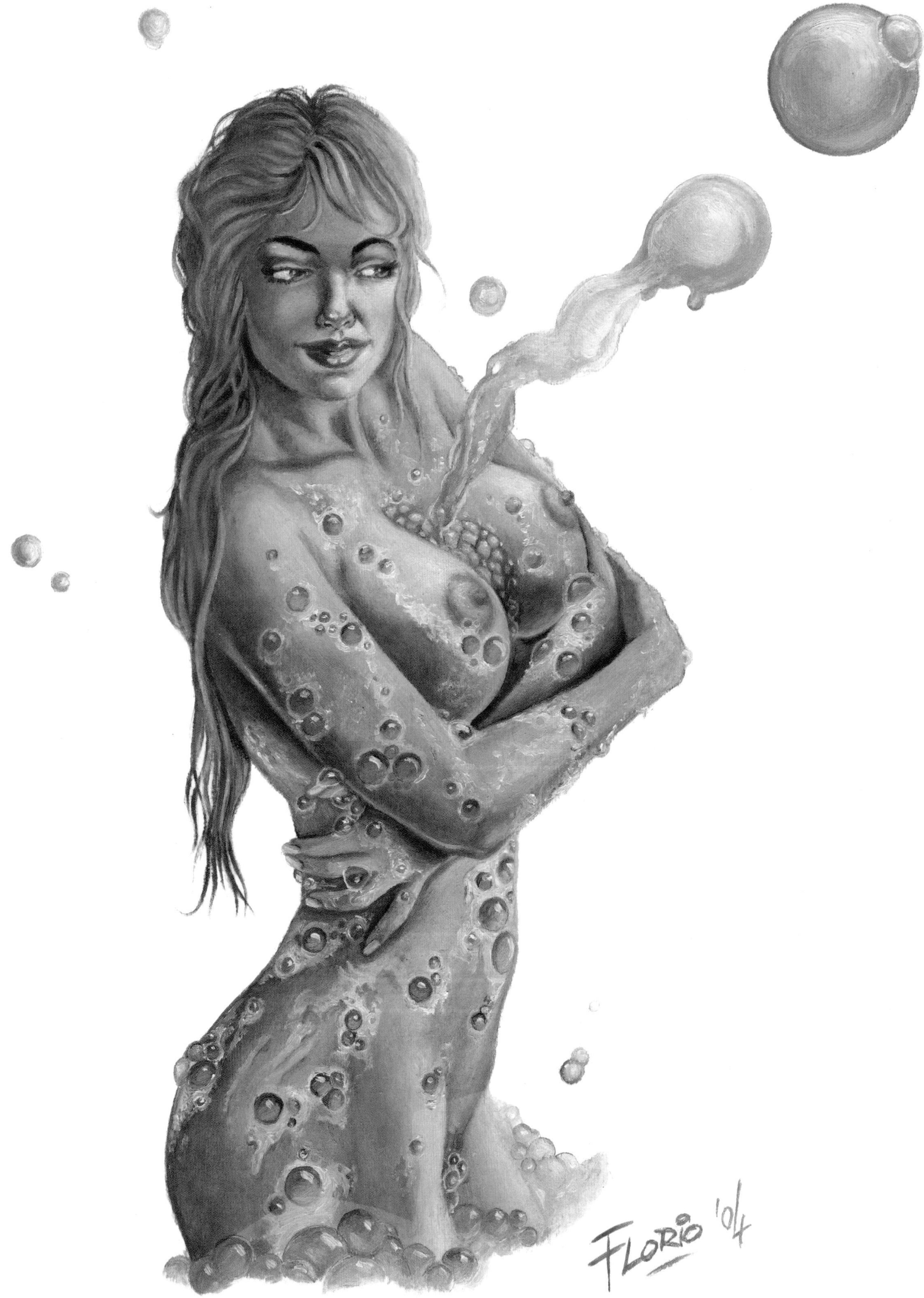
FLORIO '04

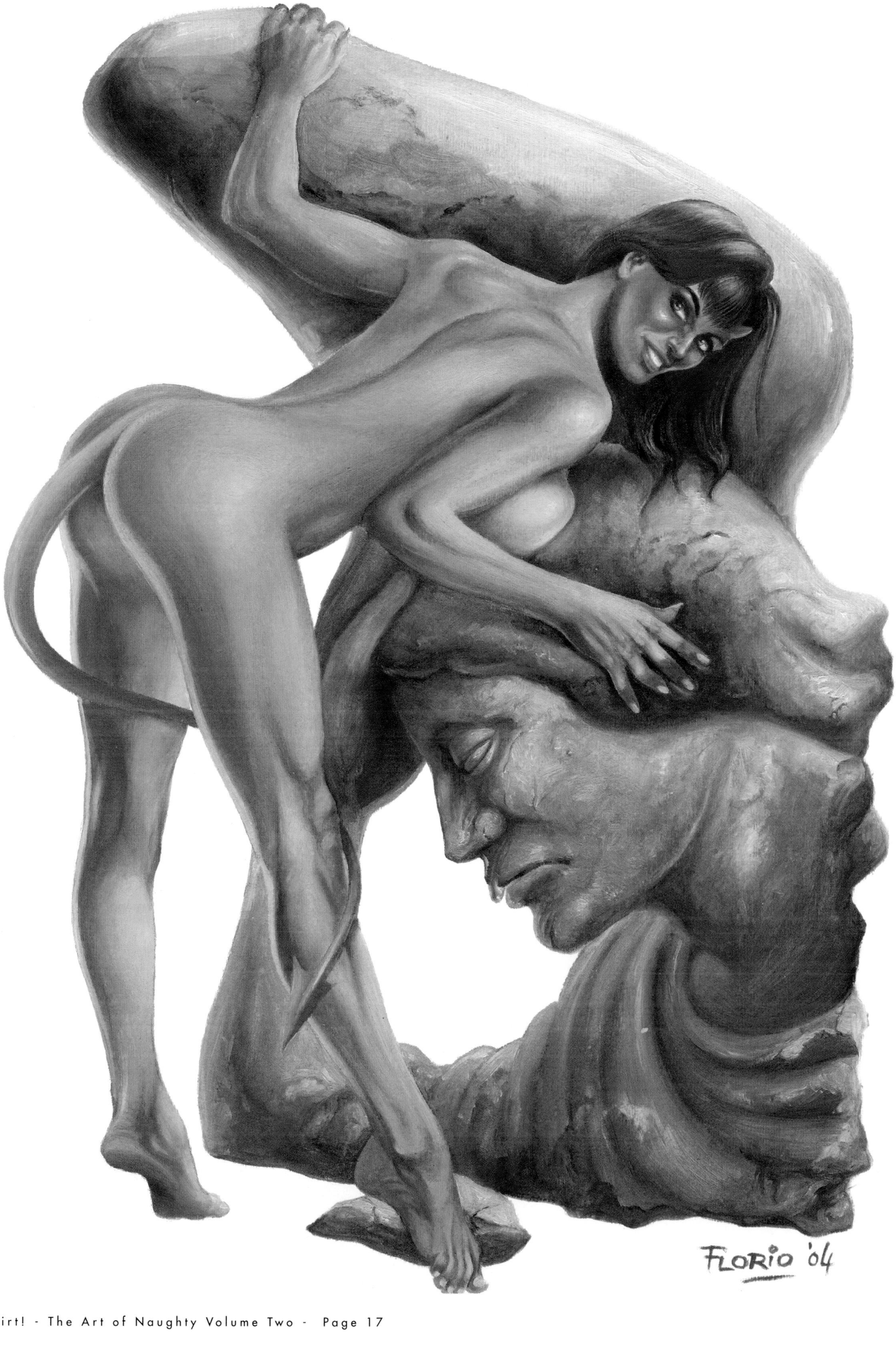
FLORIO '04

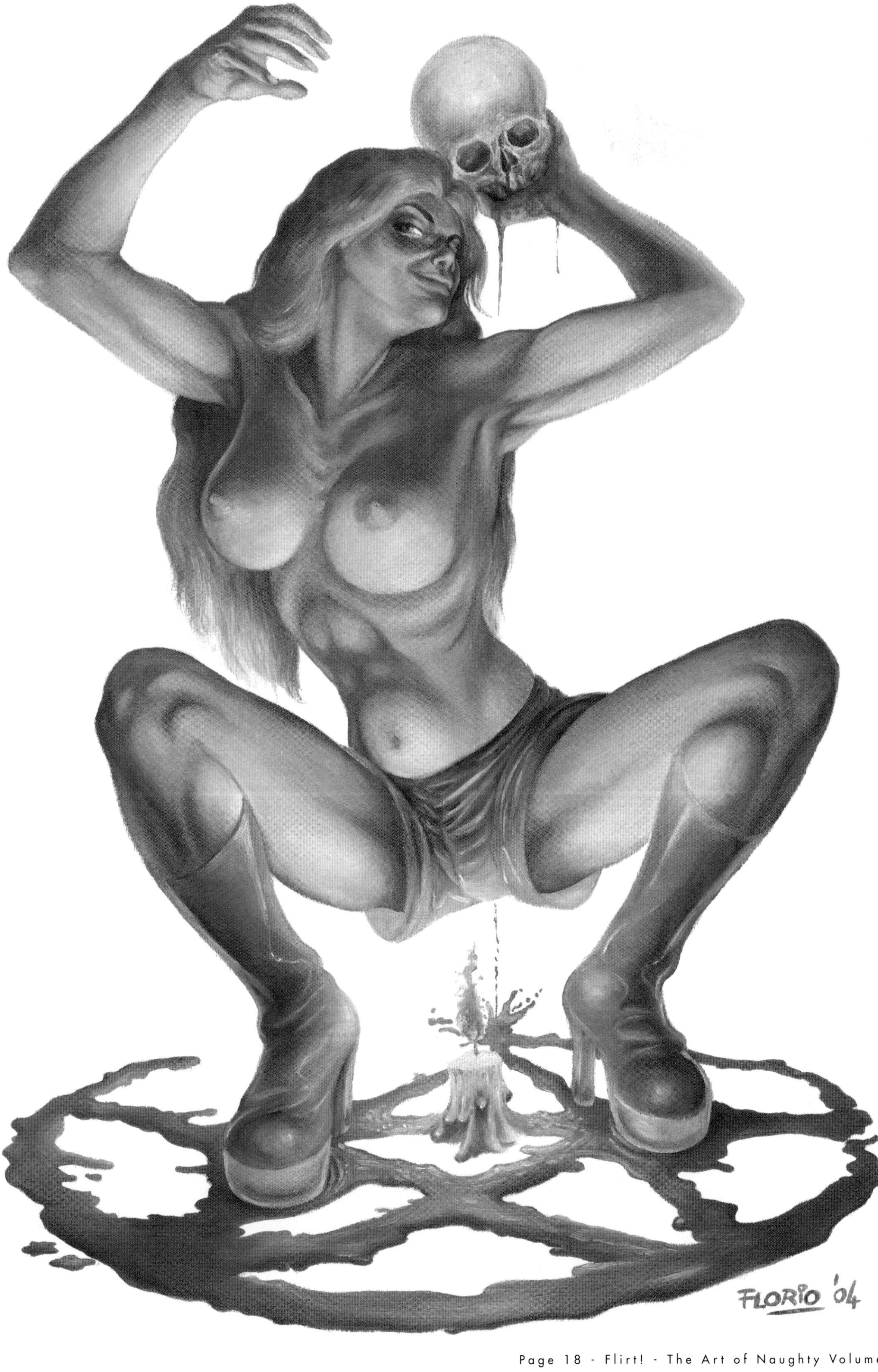
FLORIO '04

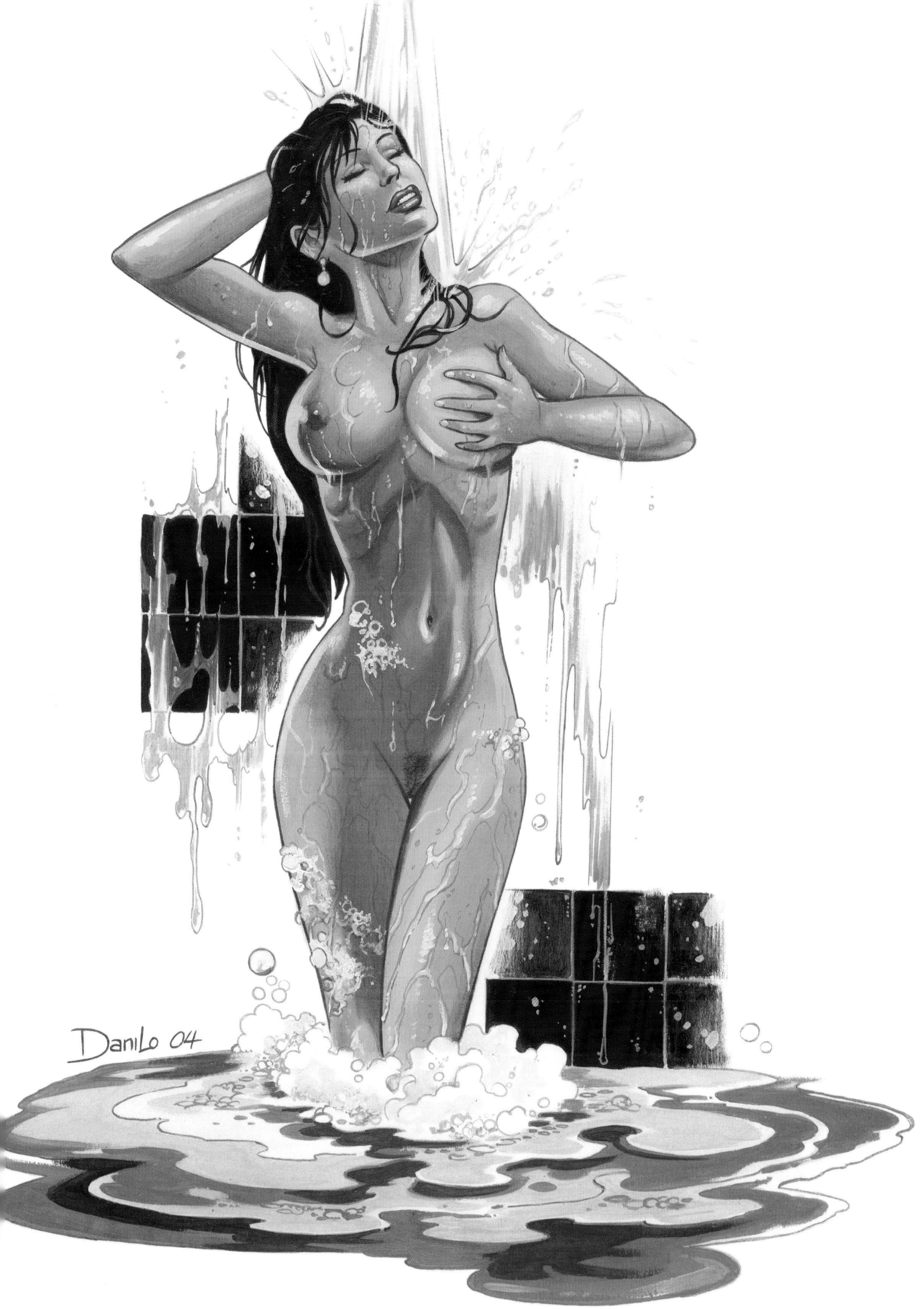
DaniLo 04

Artwork by Danilo Guida

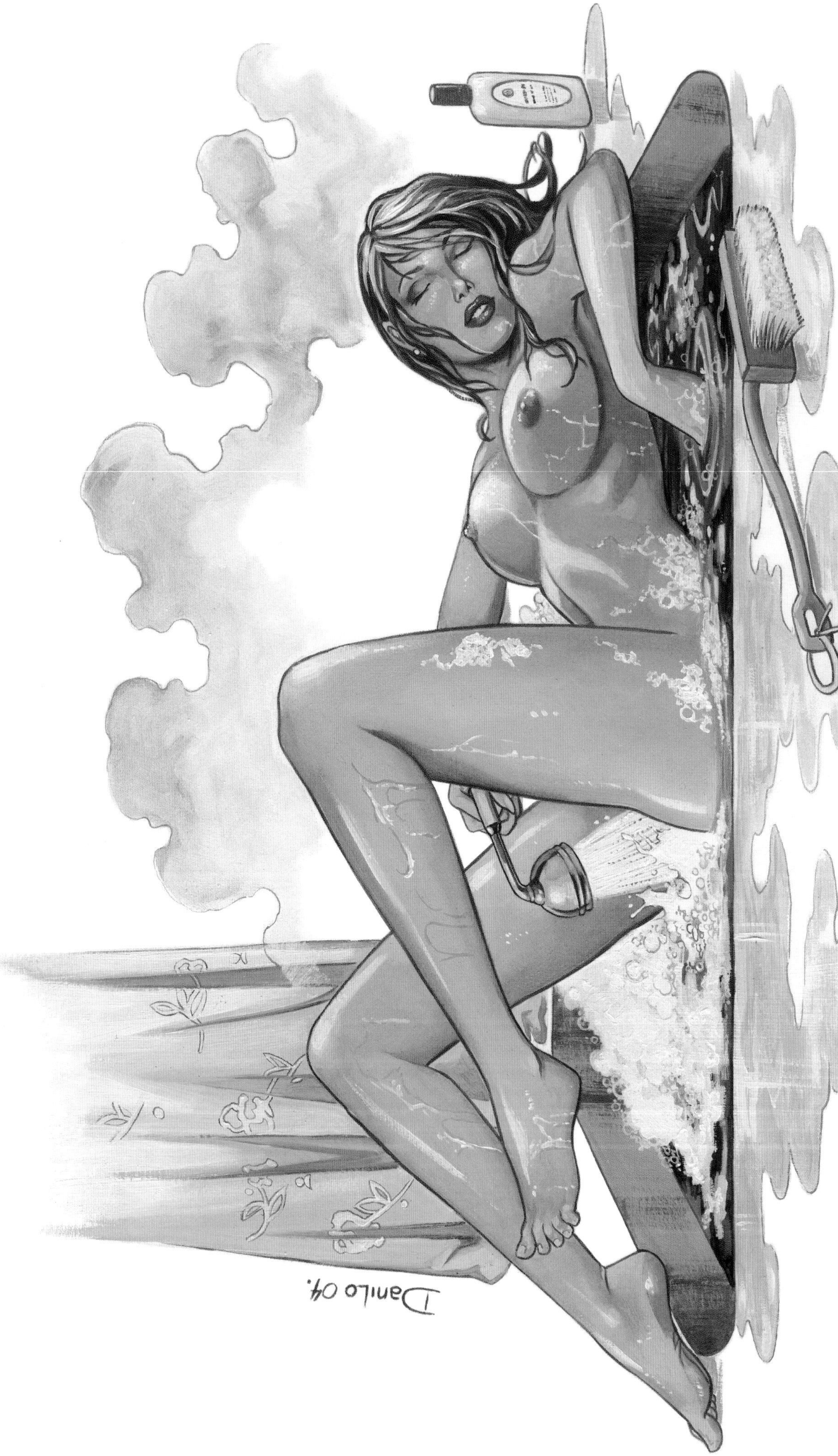
Danilo 04.

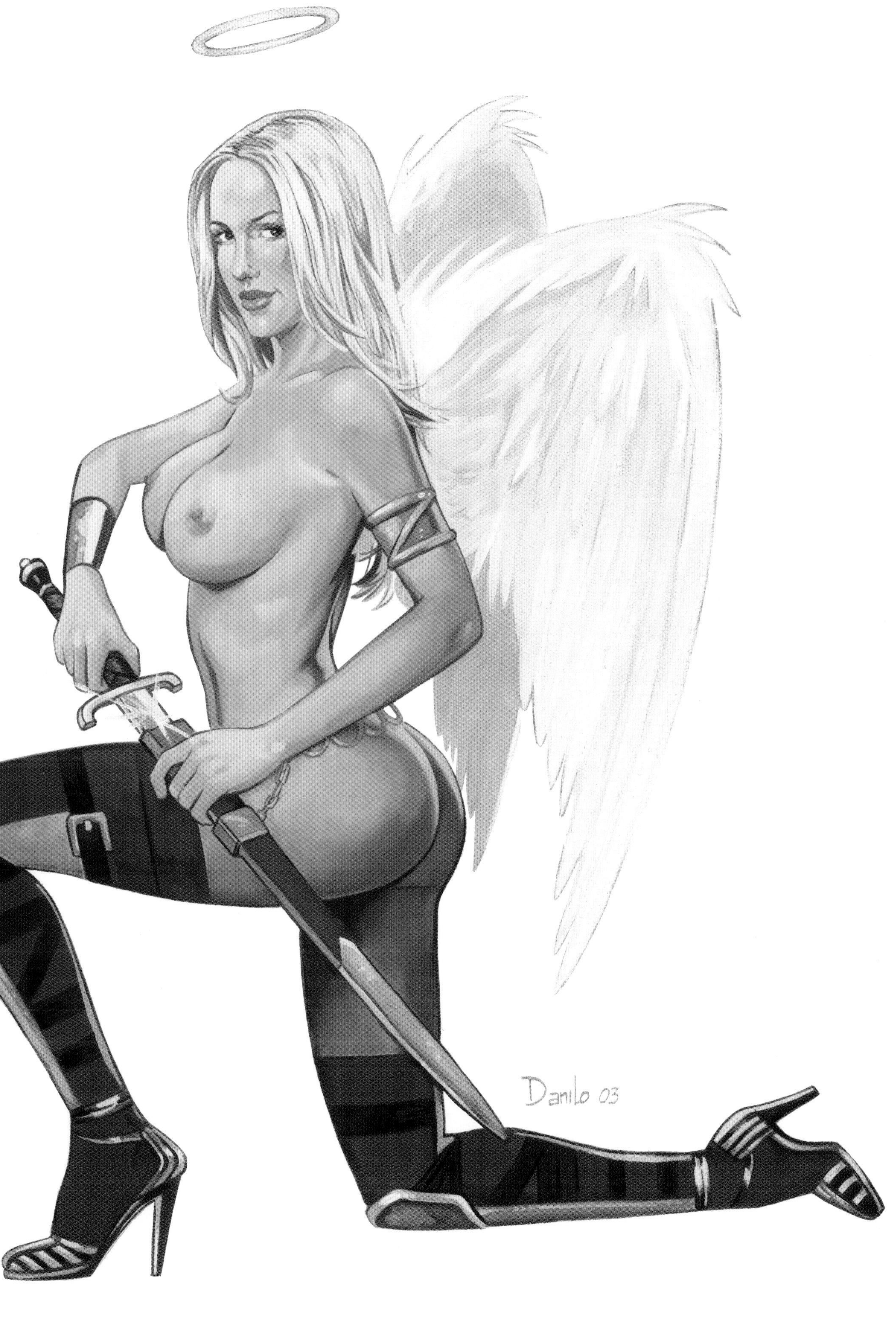
Danilo 03

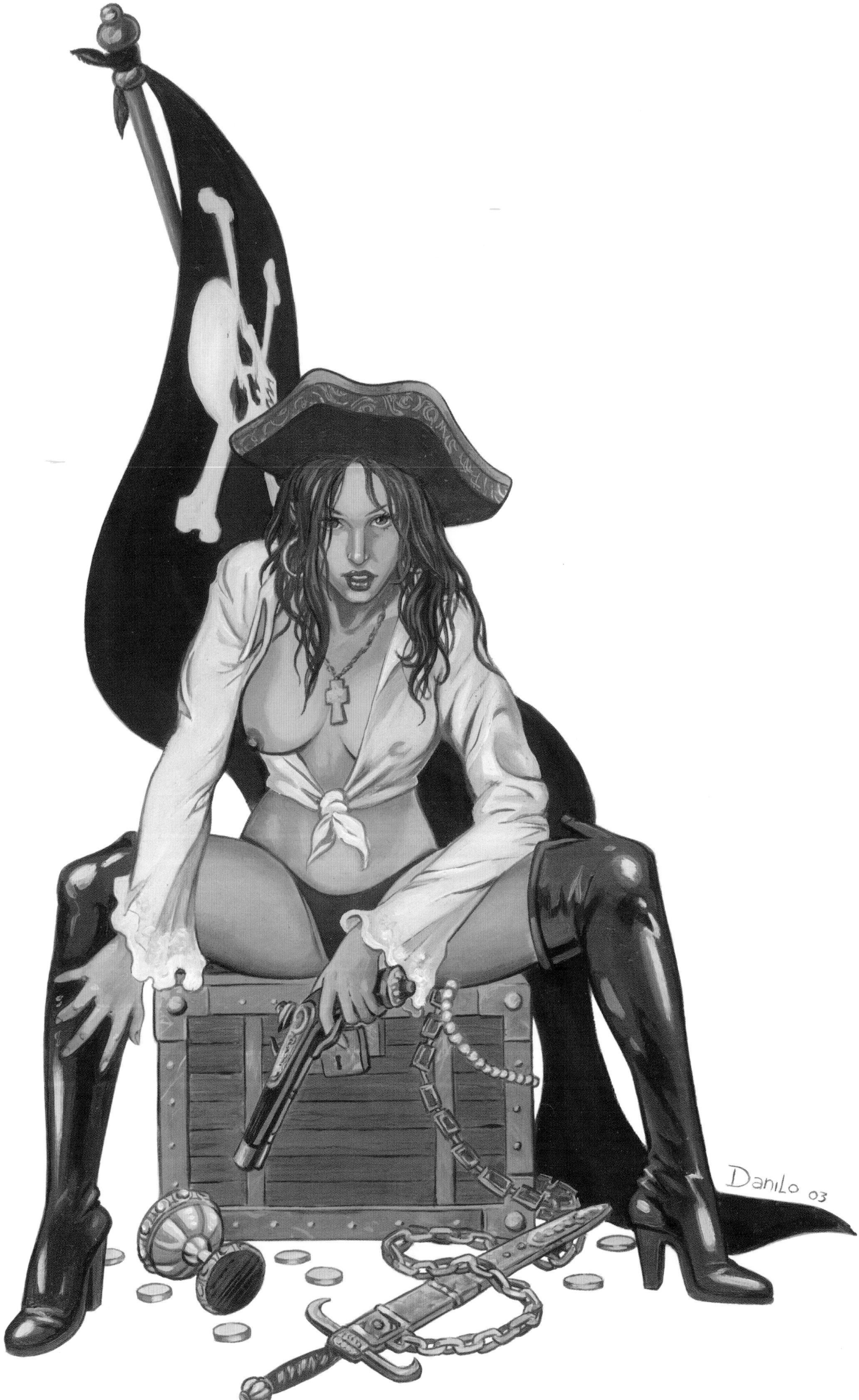
DaniLo 03

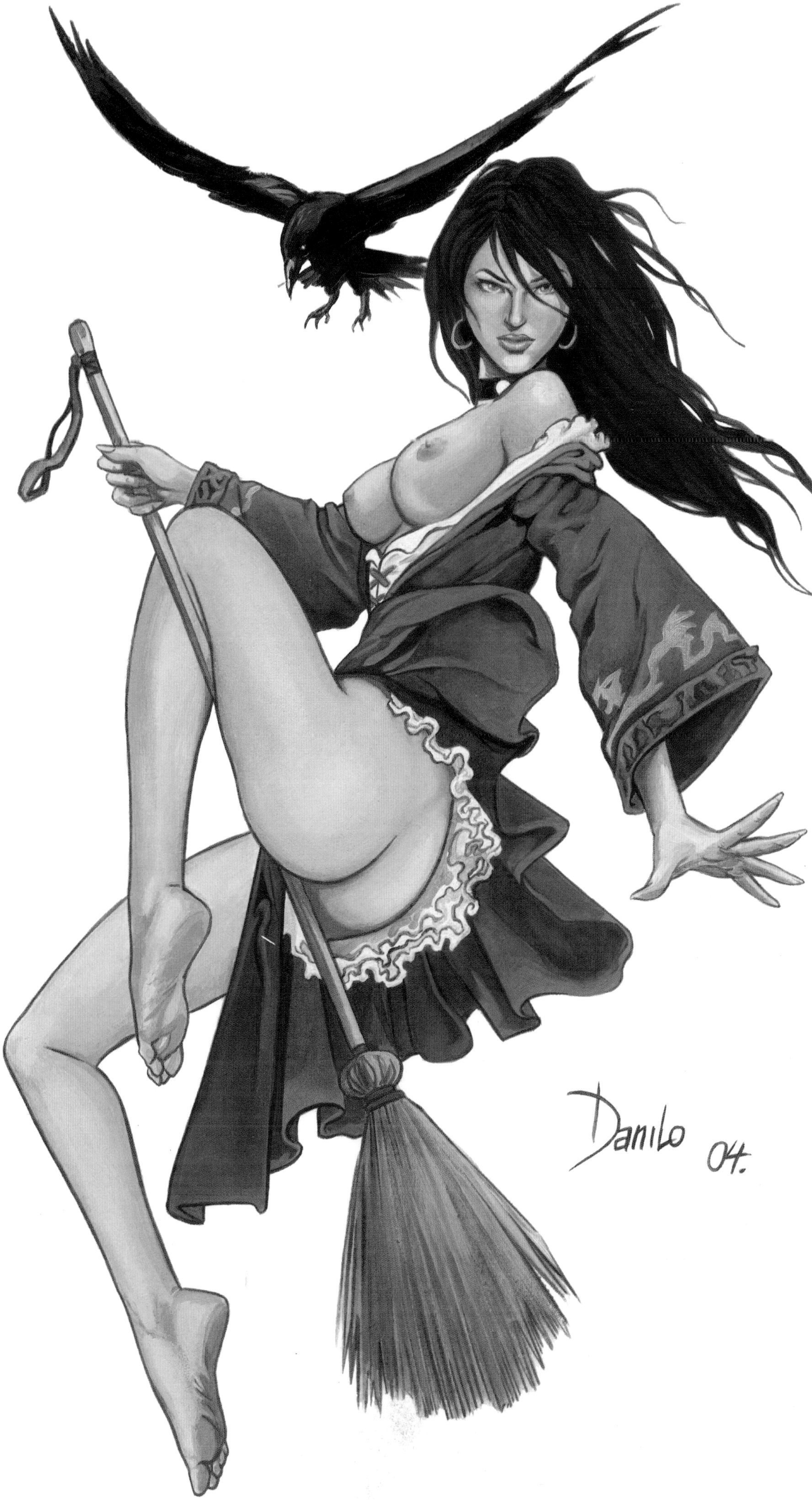
Danilo 04.

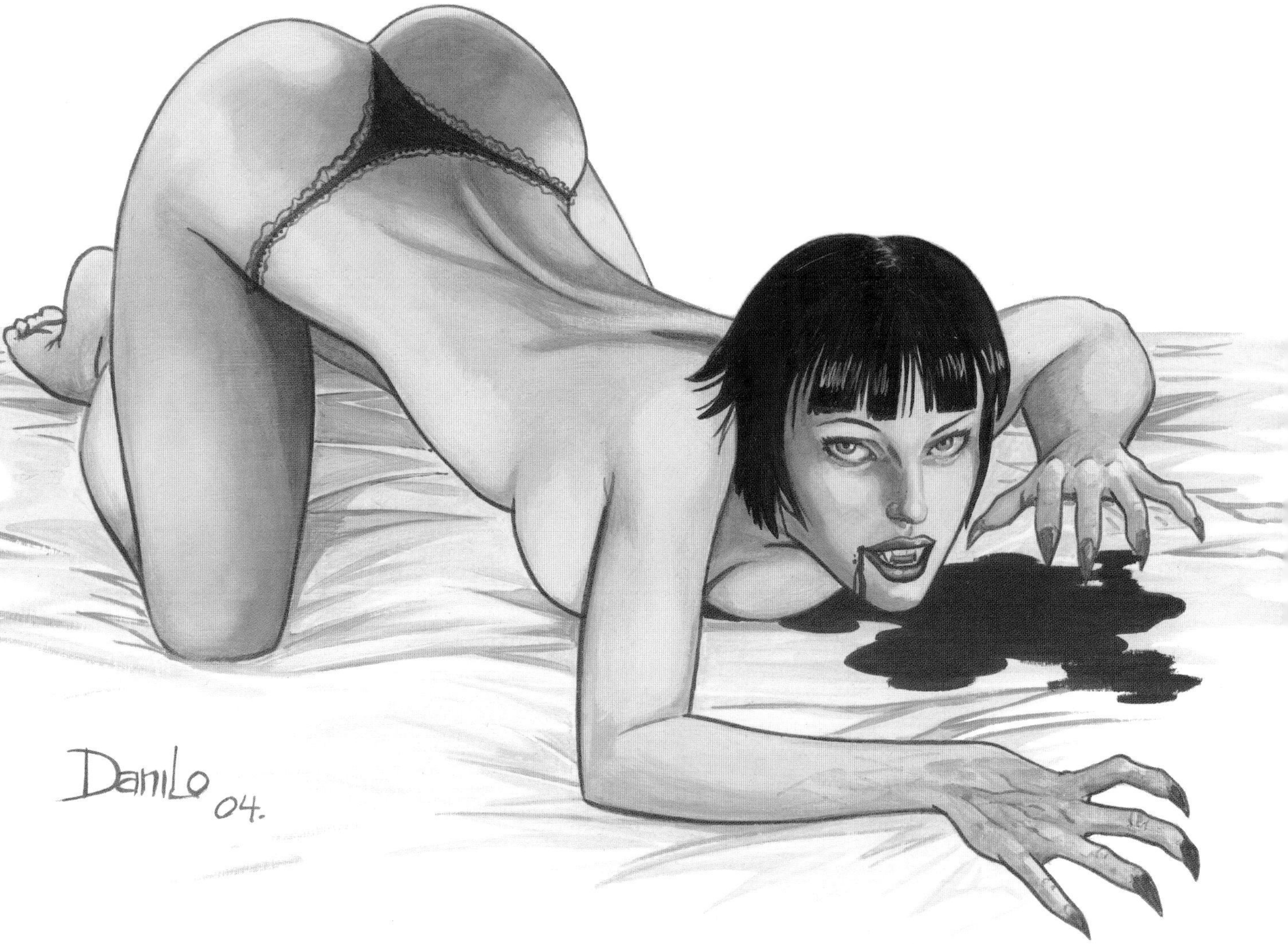
DaniLo 04.

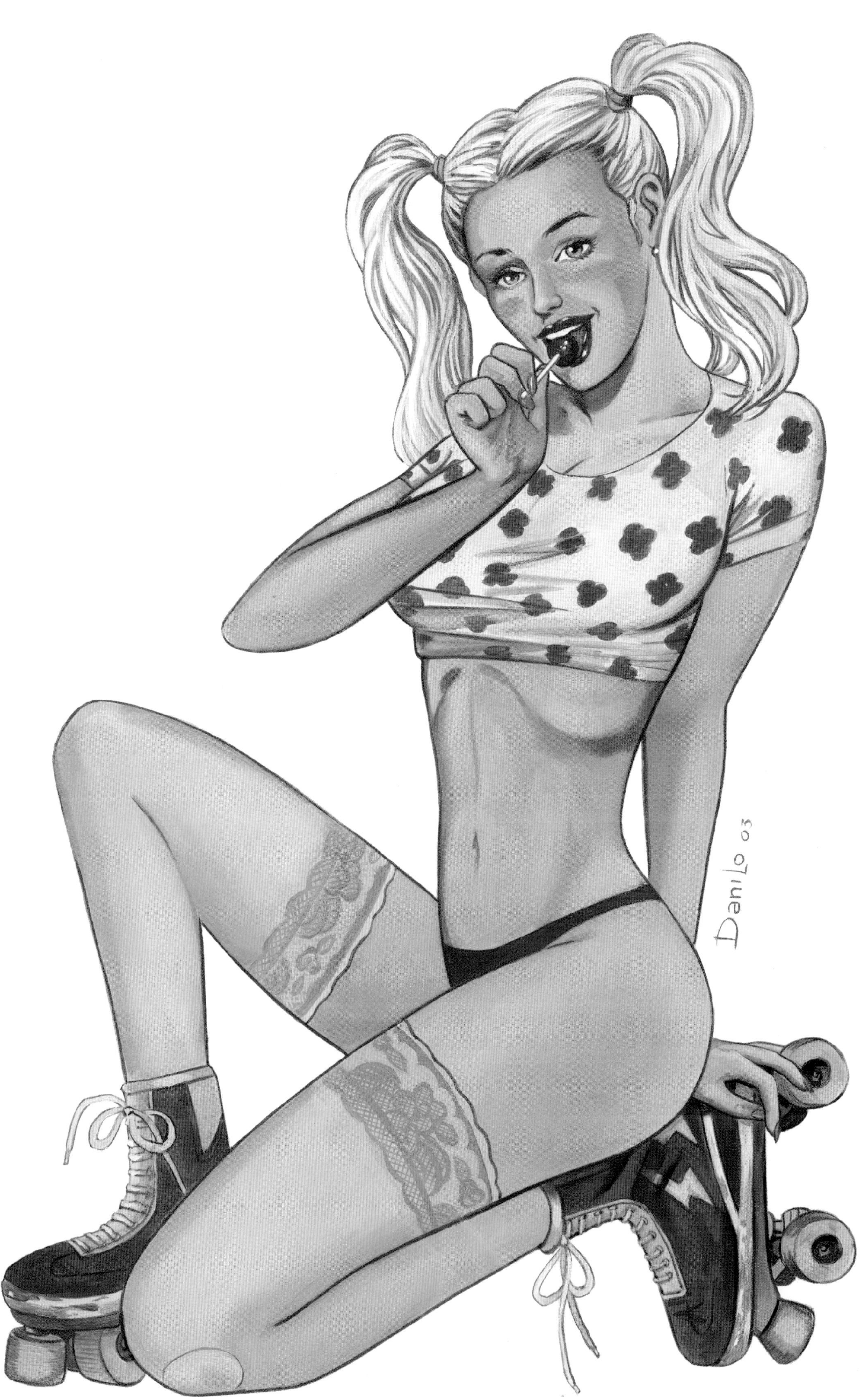
DaniLo 03

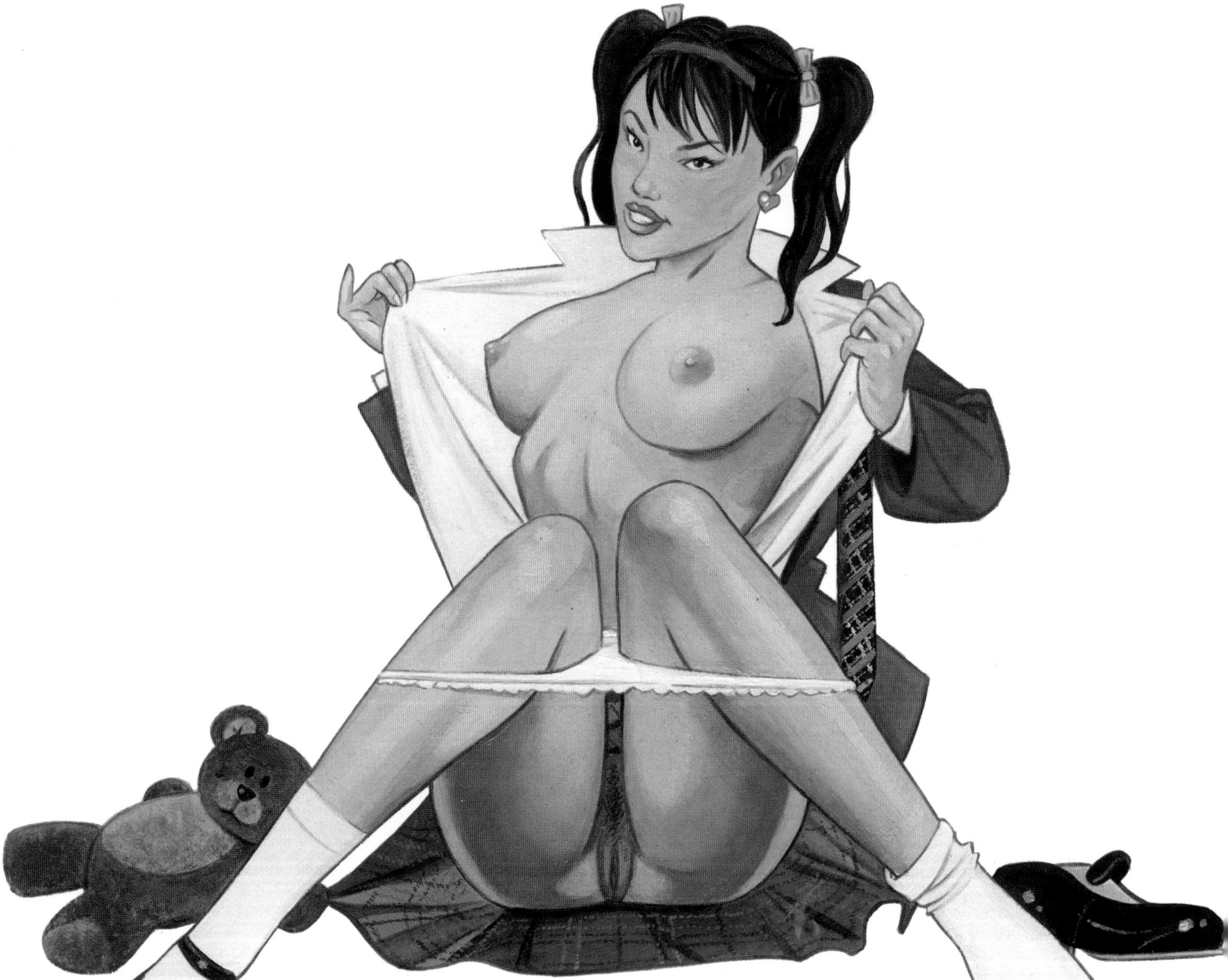
Danilo 04.

Danilo 04.

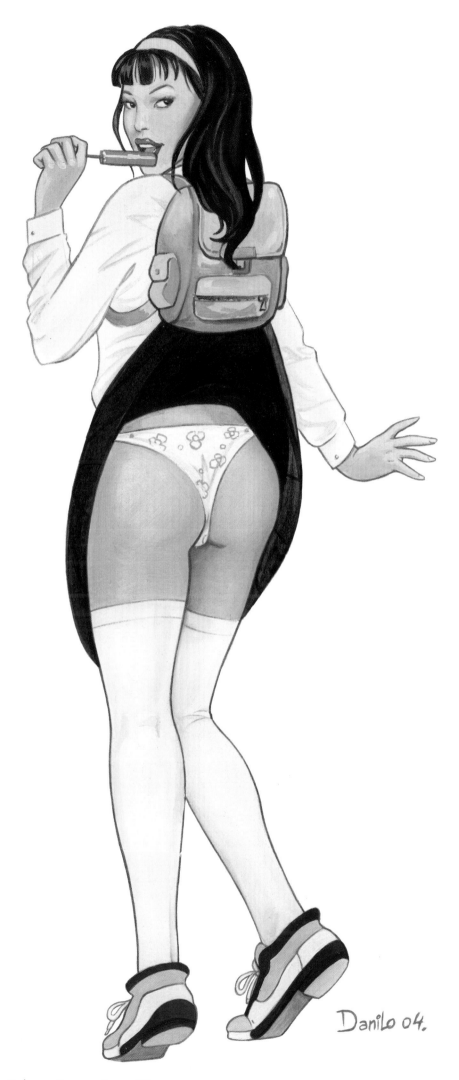

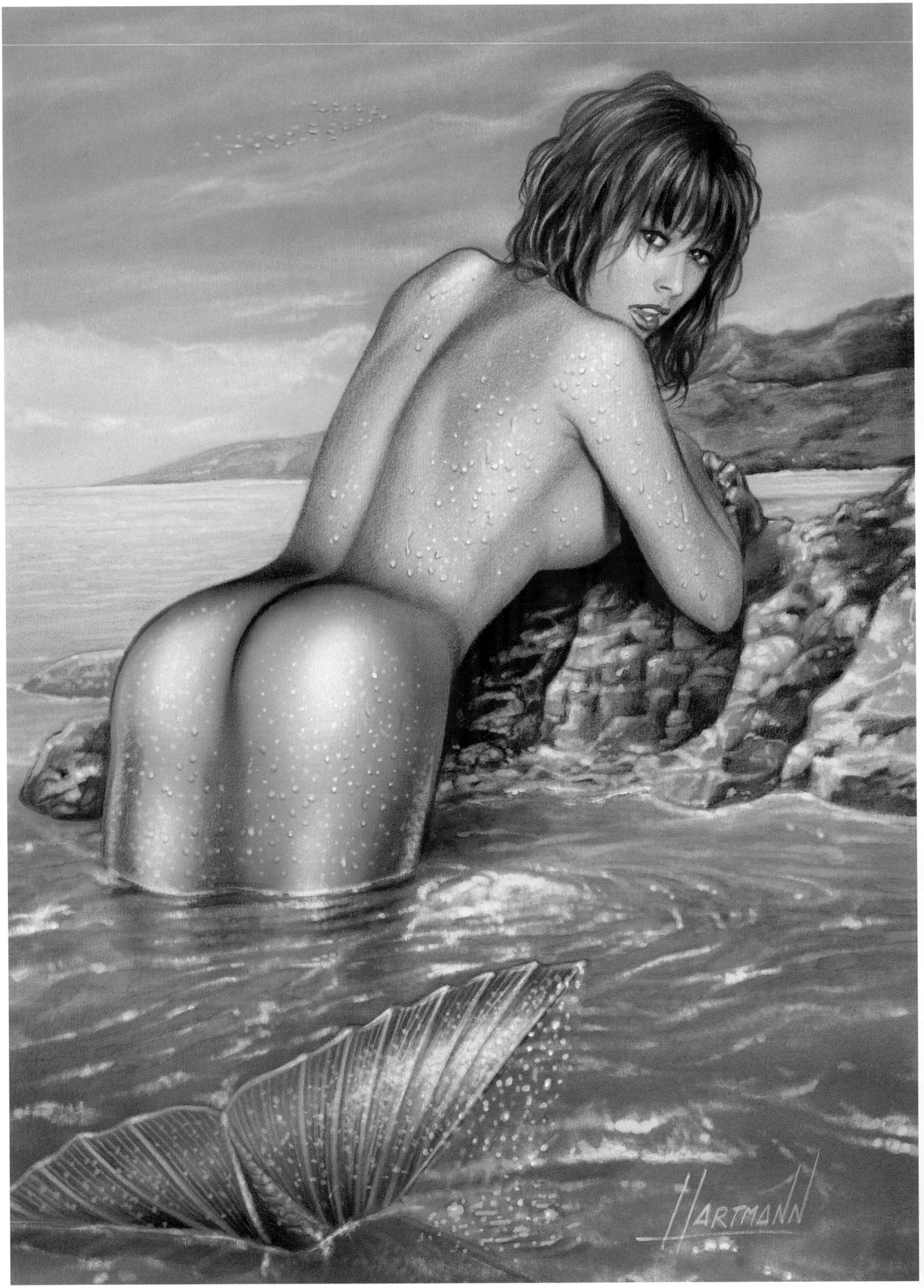
HARTMANN

Artwork by Dario Hartmann

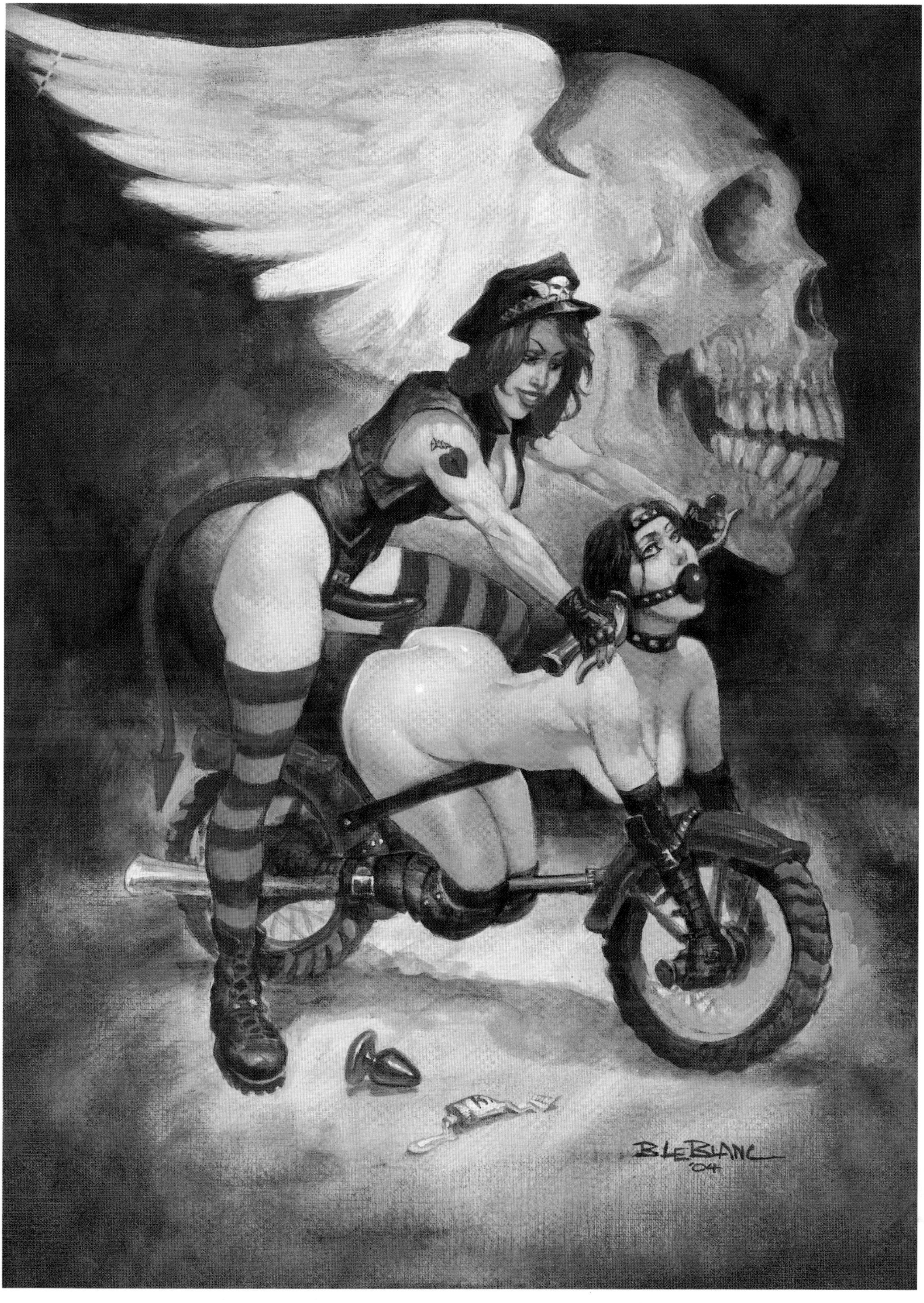

B LEBLANC
'04

Artwork by Brian LeBlanc

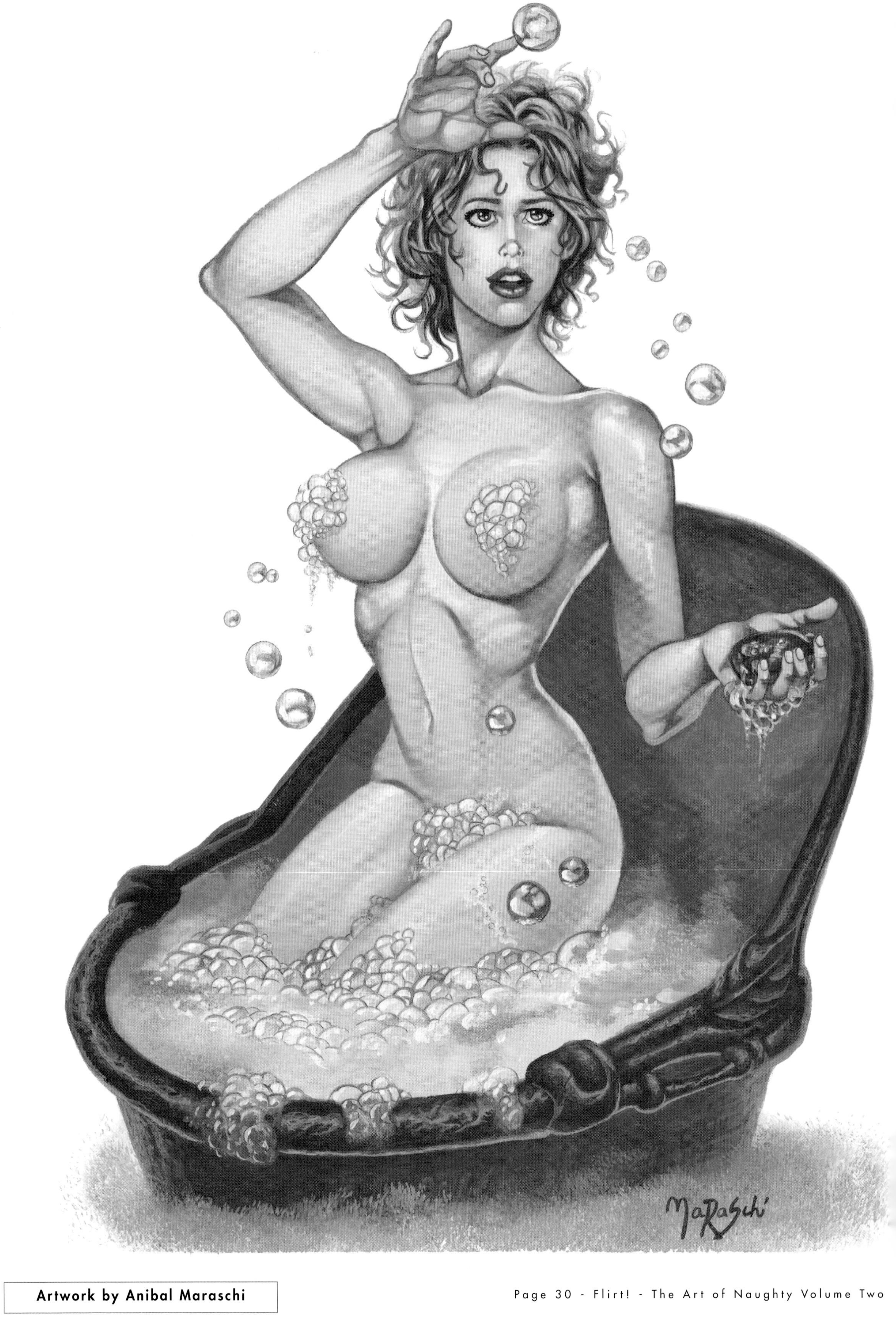

Artwork by Anibal Maraschi

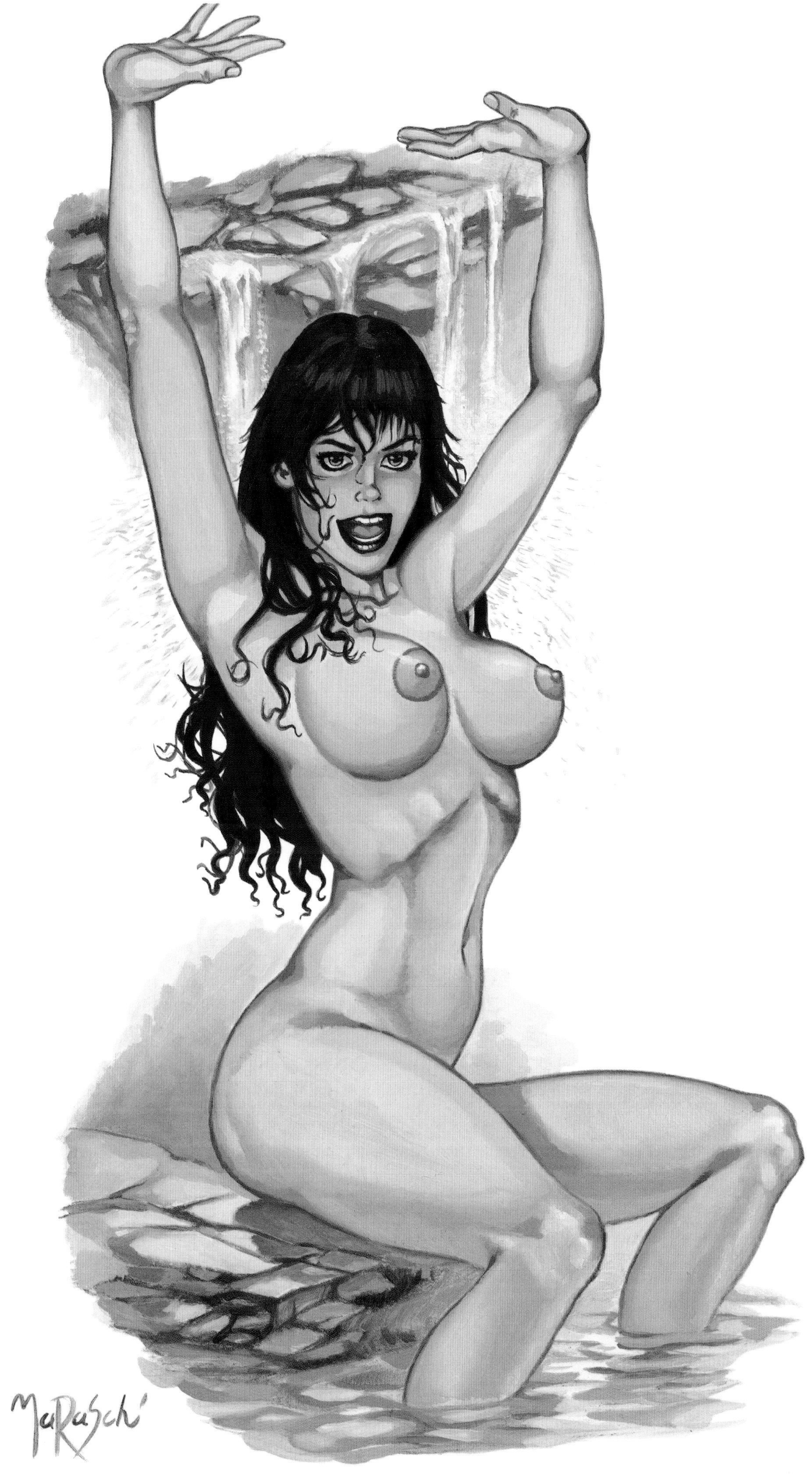

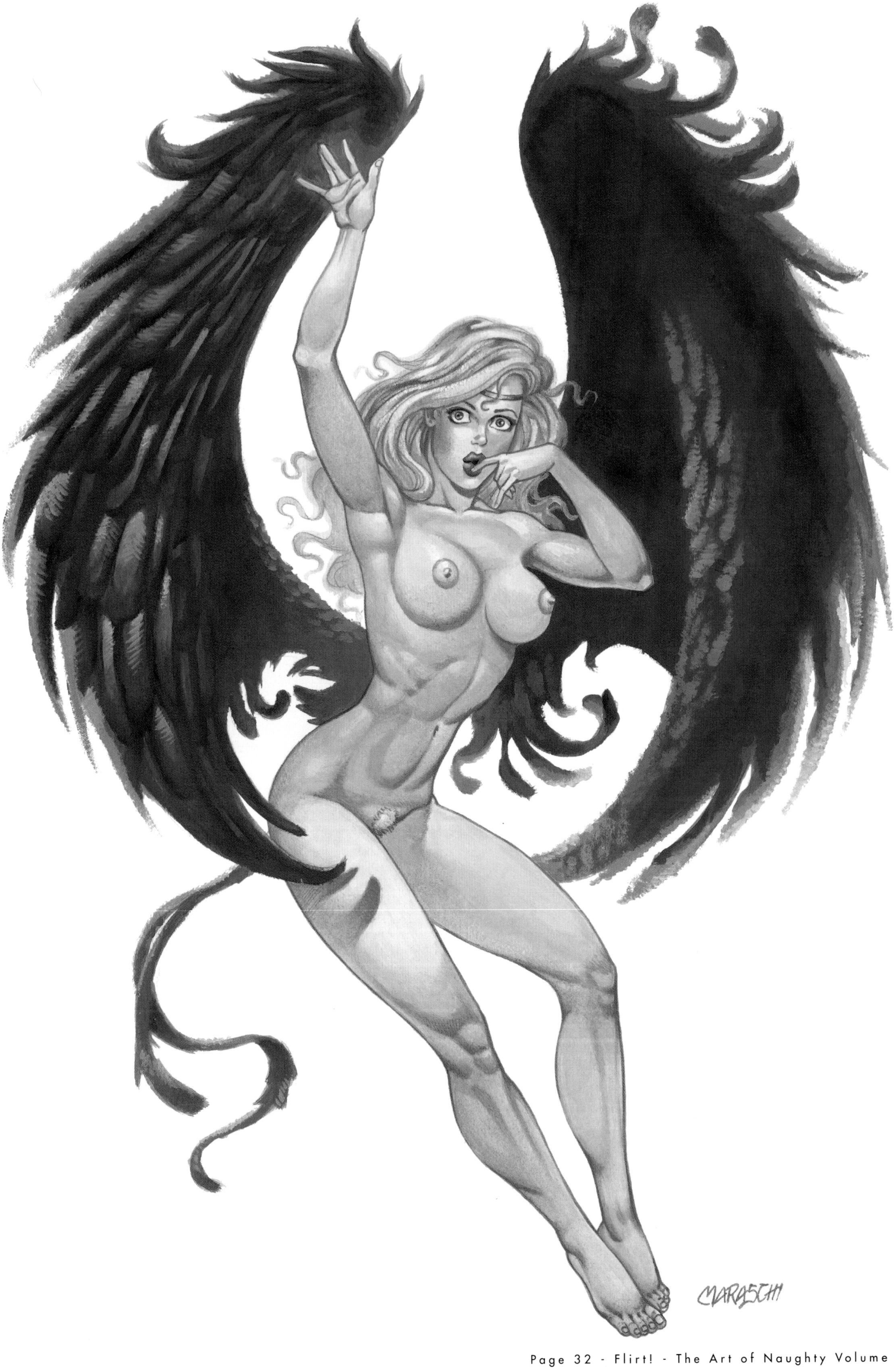
MARASCHI

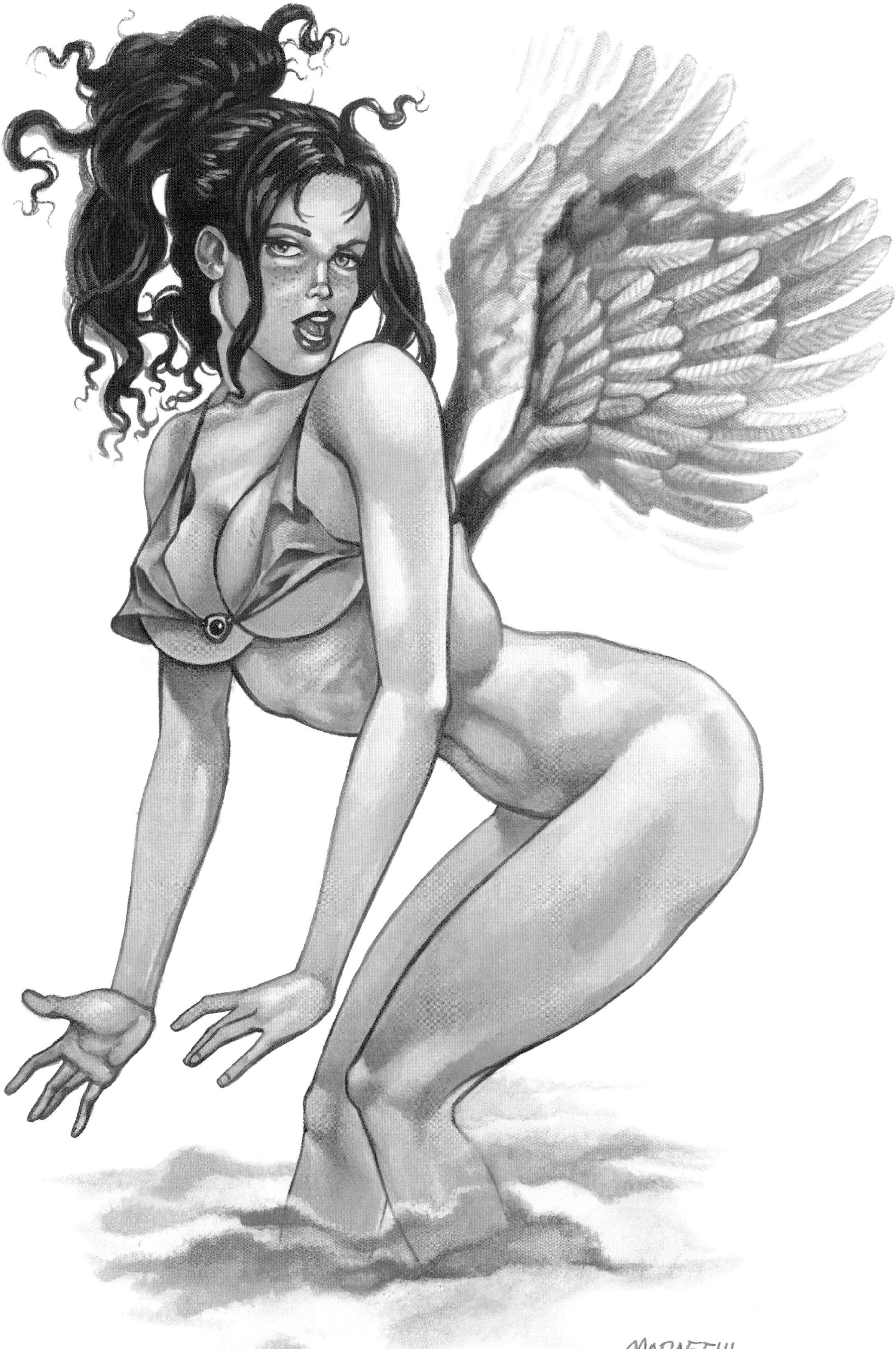
MARASCHI

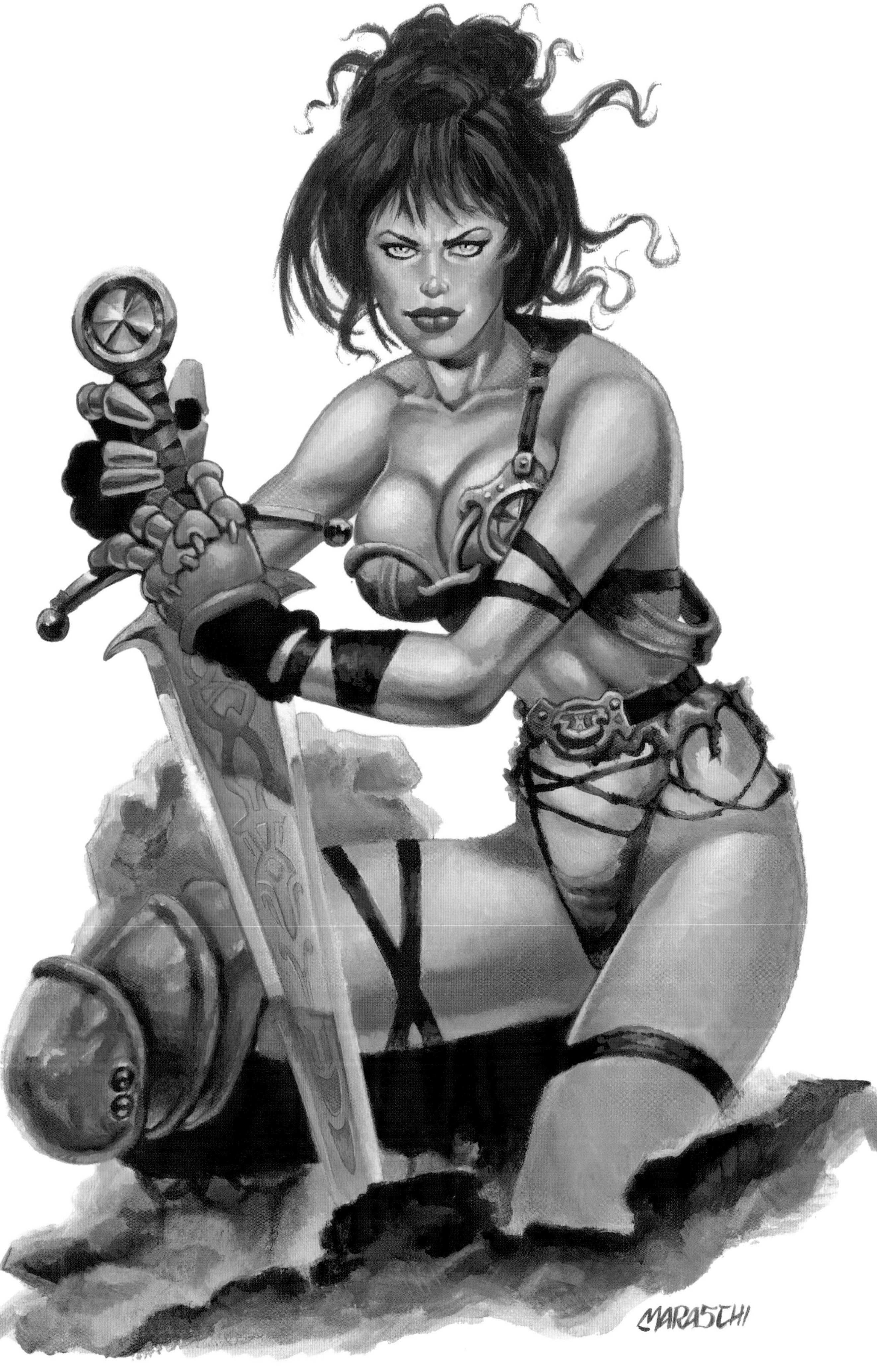
MARASCHI

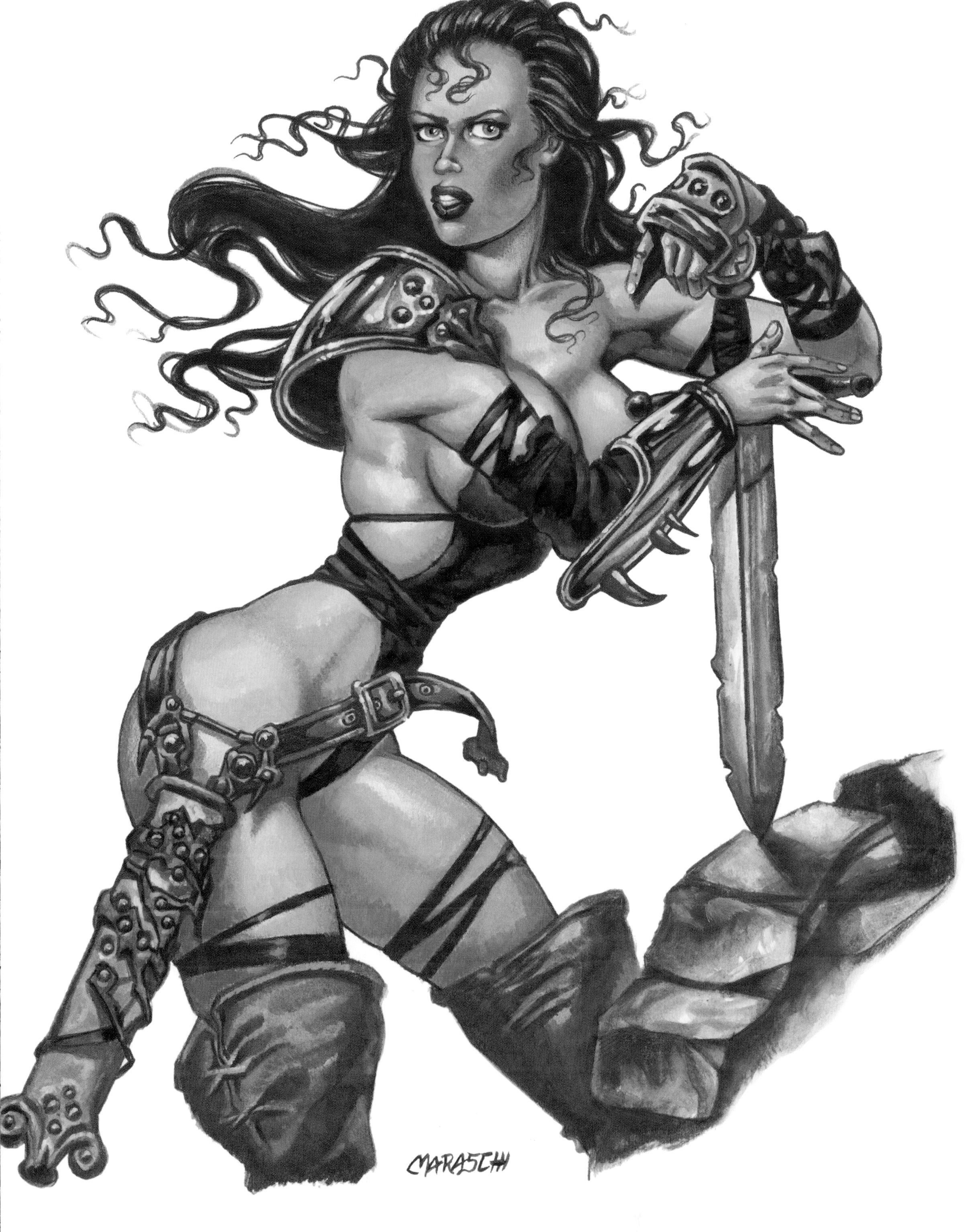
MARASCHI

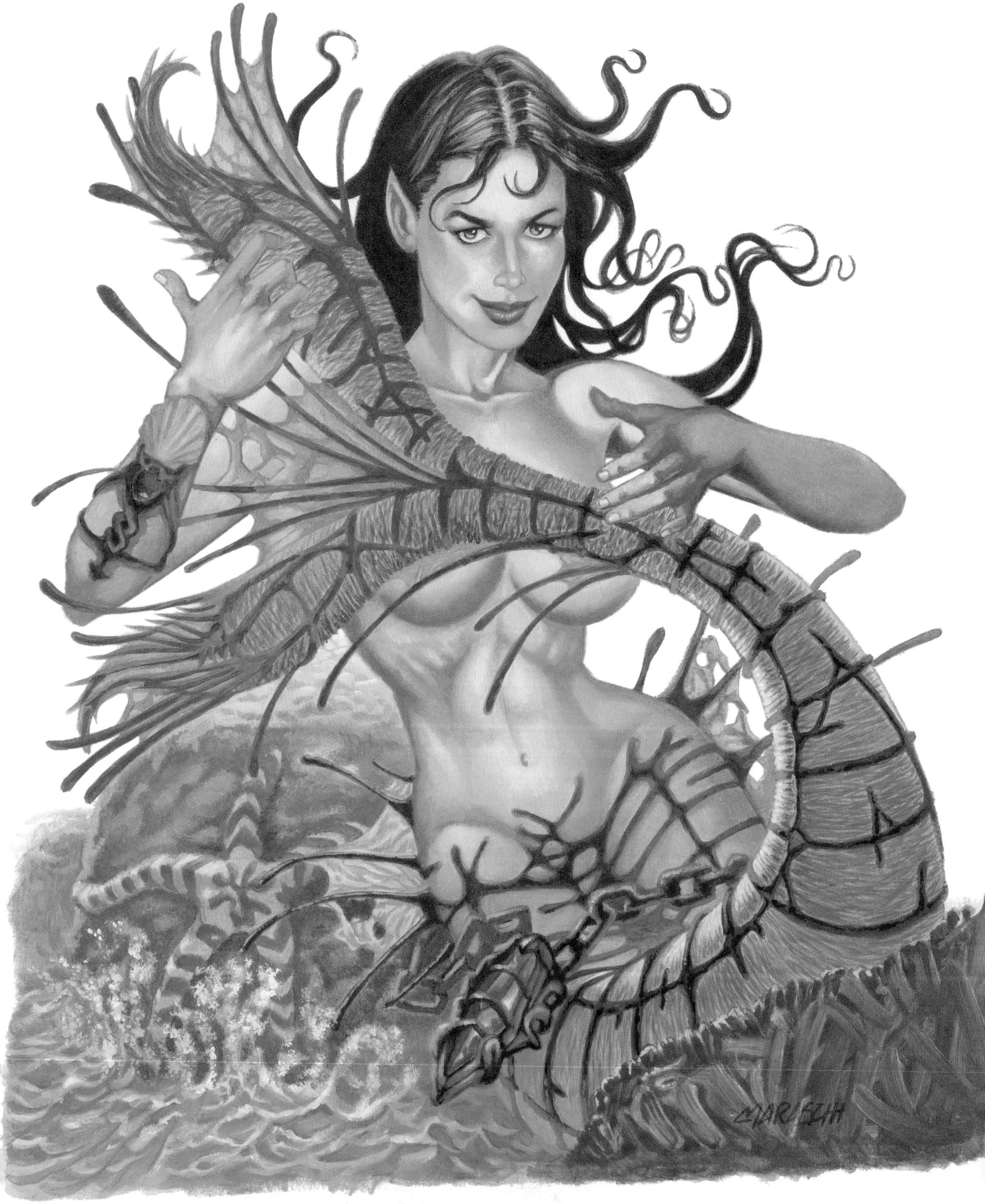
MARISSA

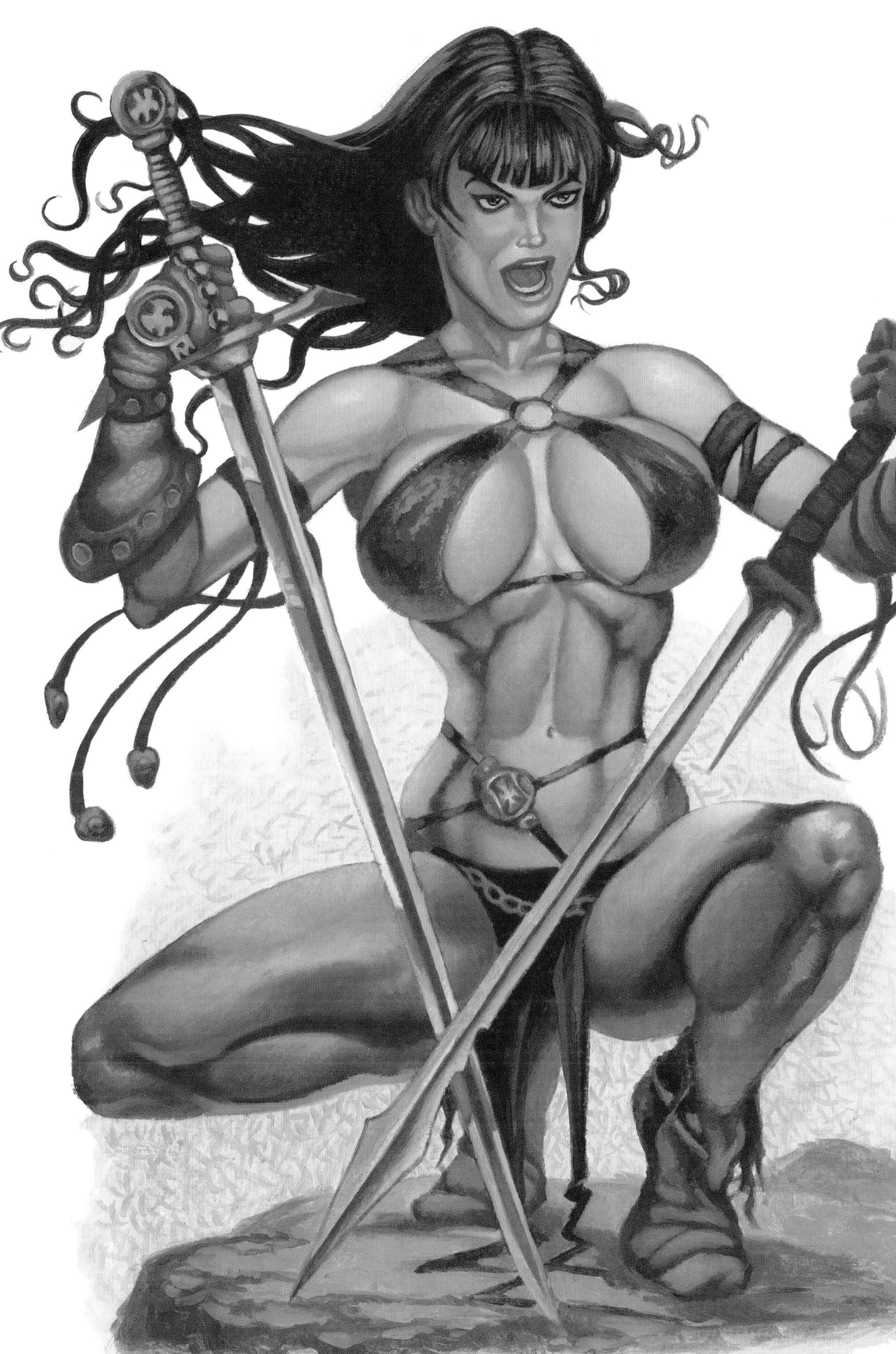

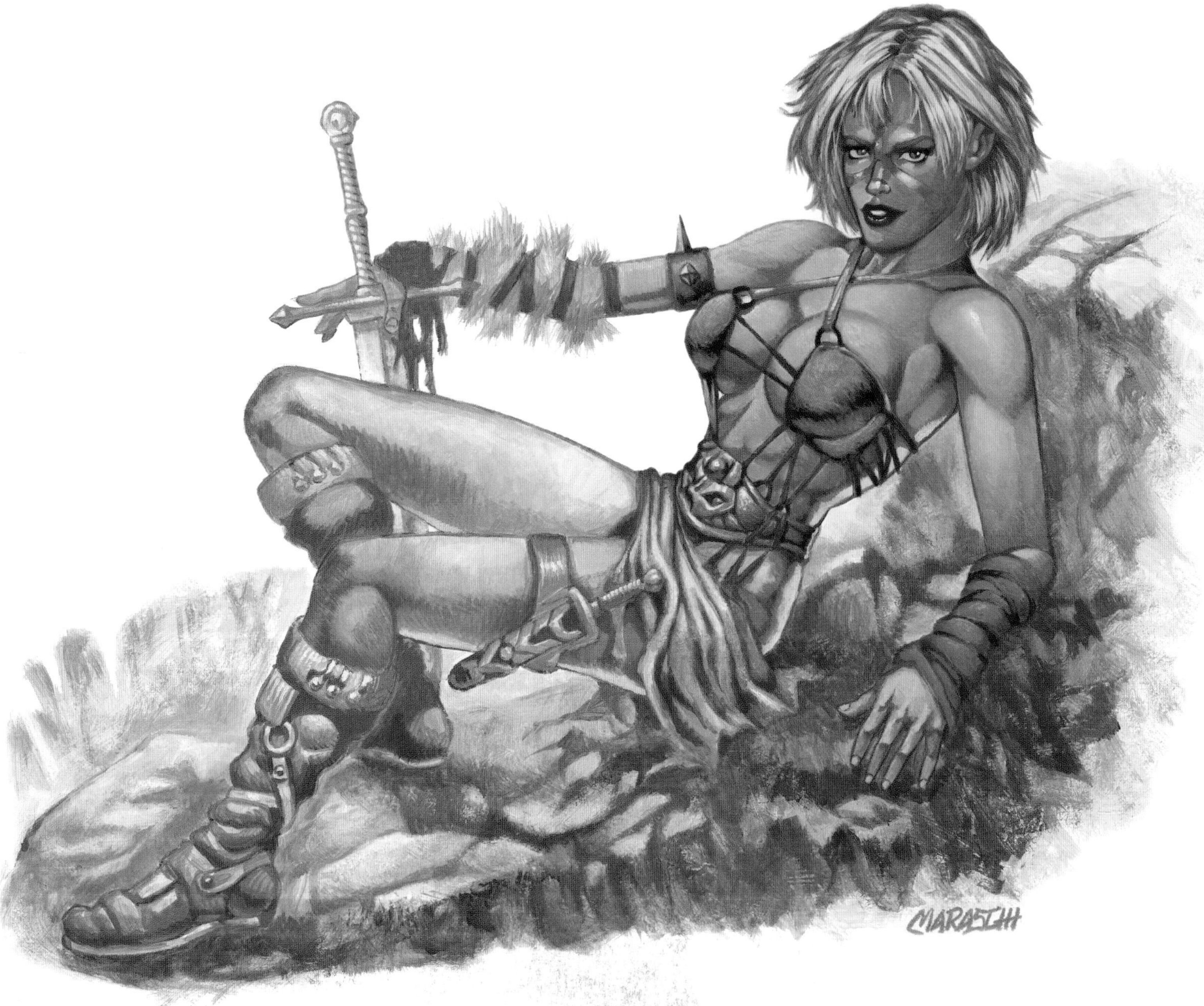
MARASCHI

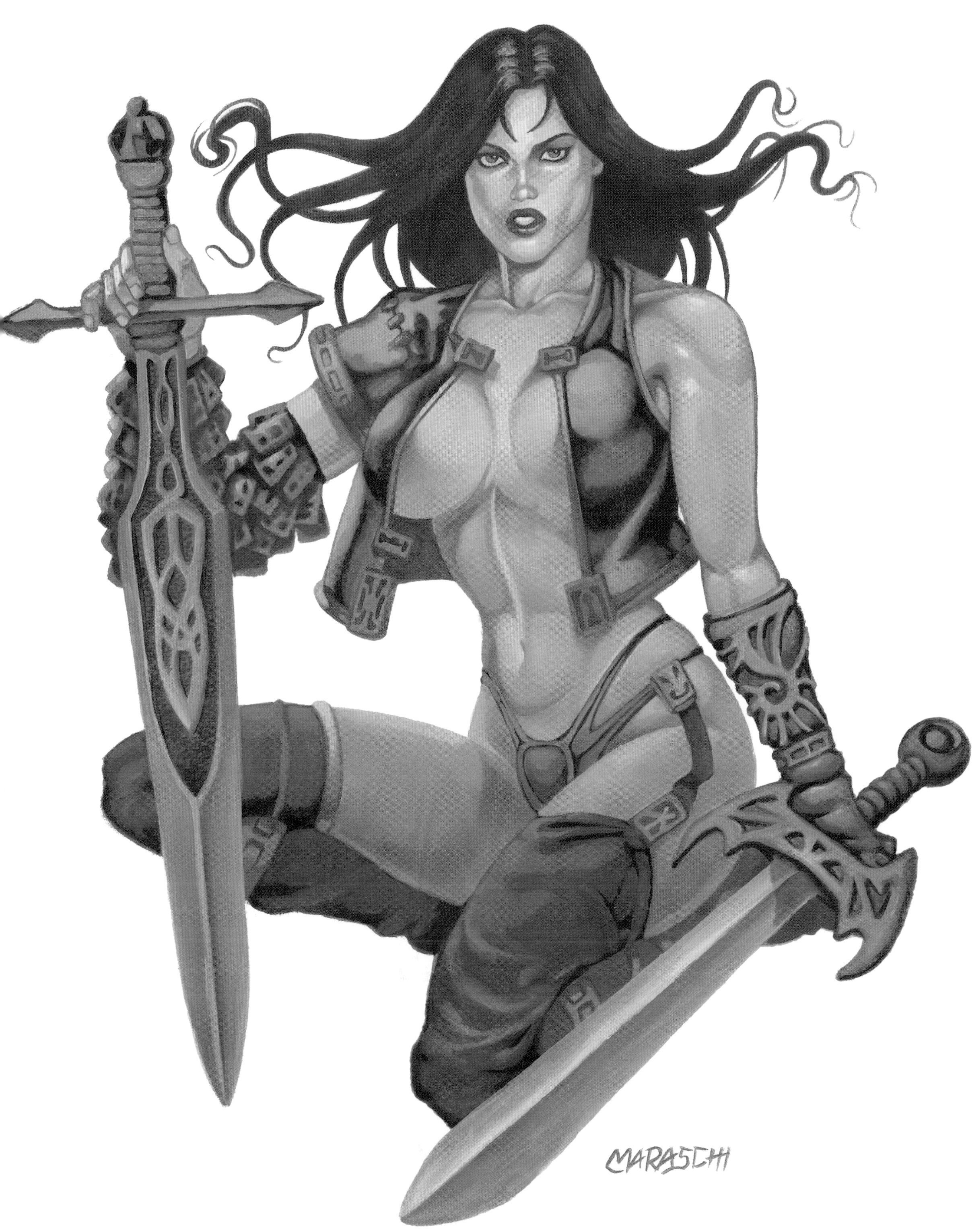
MARASCHI

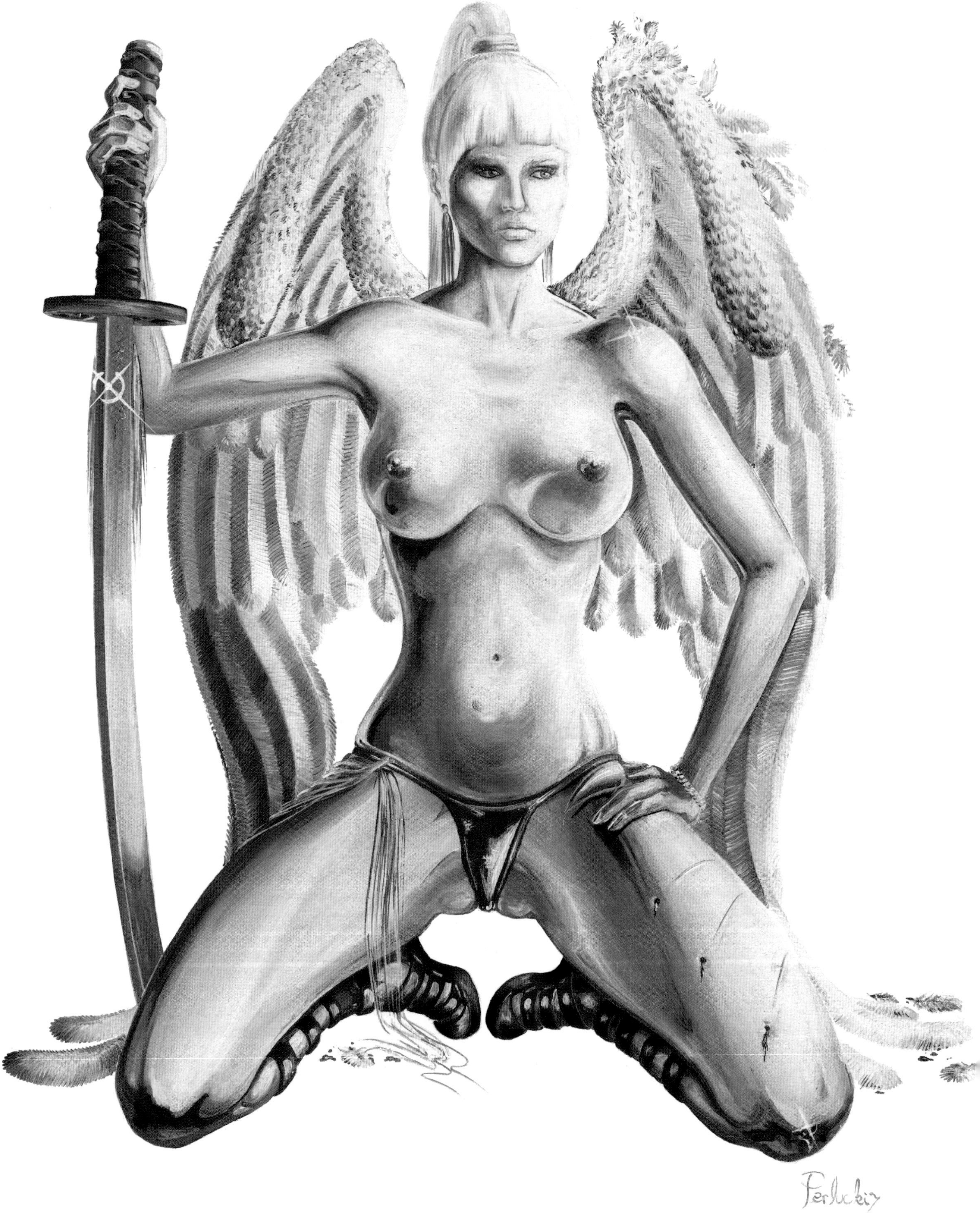
Perlucky

Artwork by Perla Perlucky

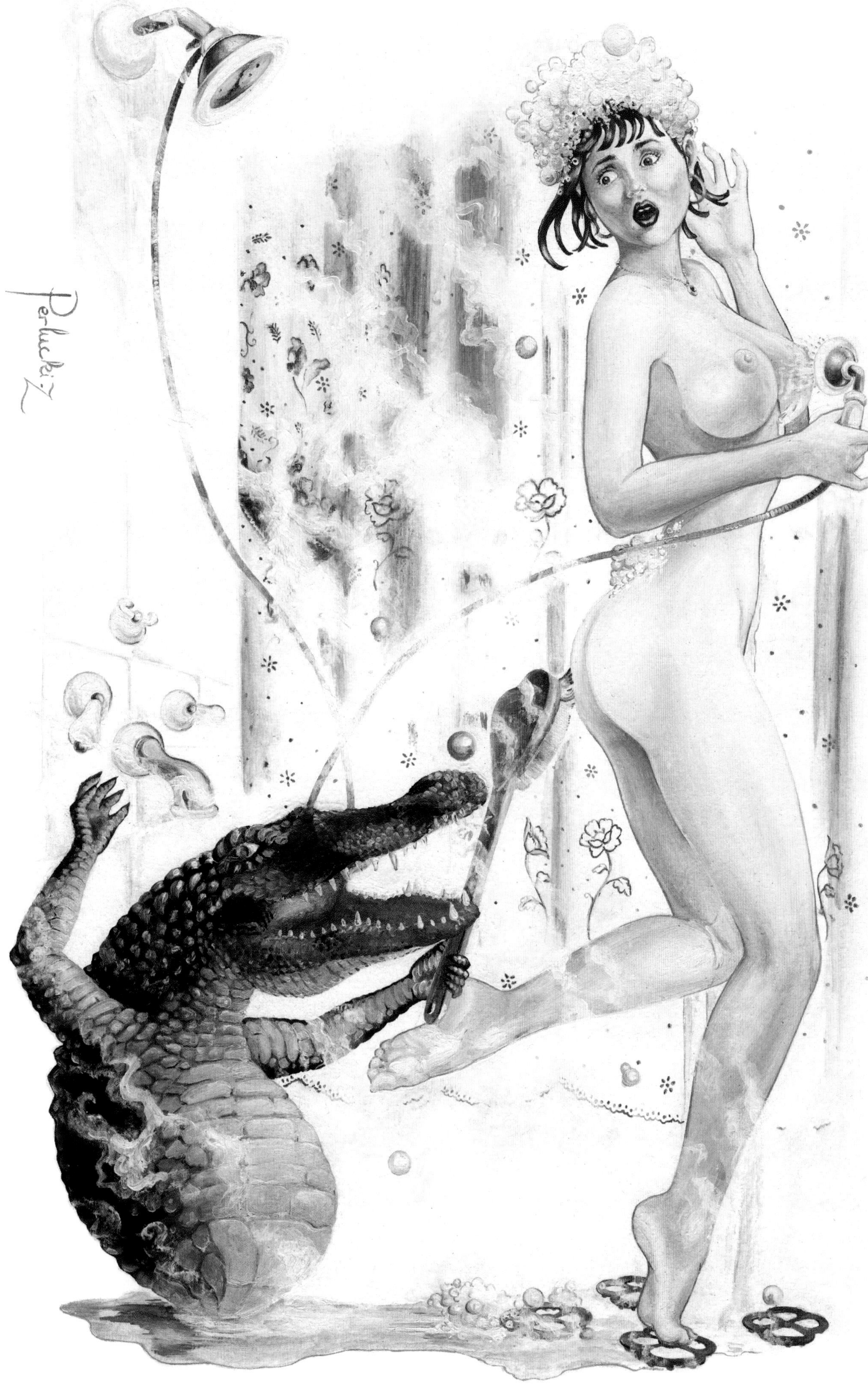

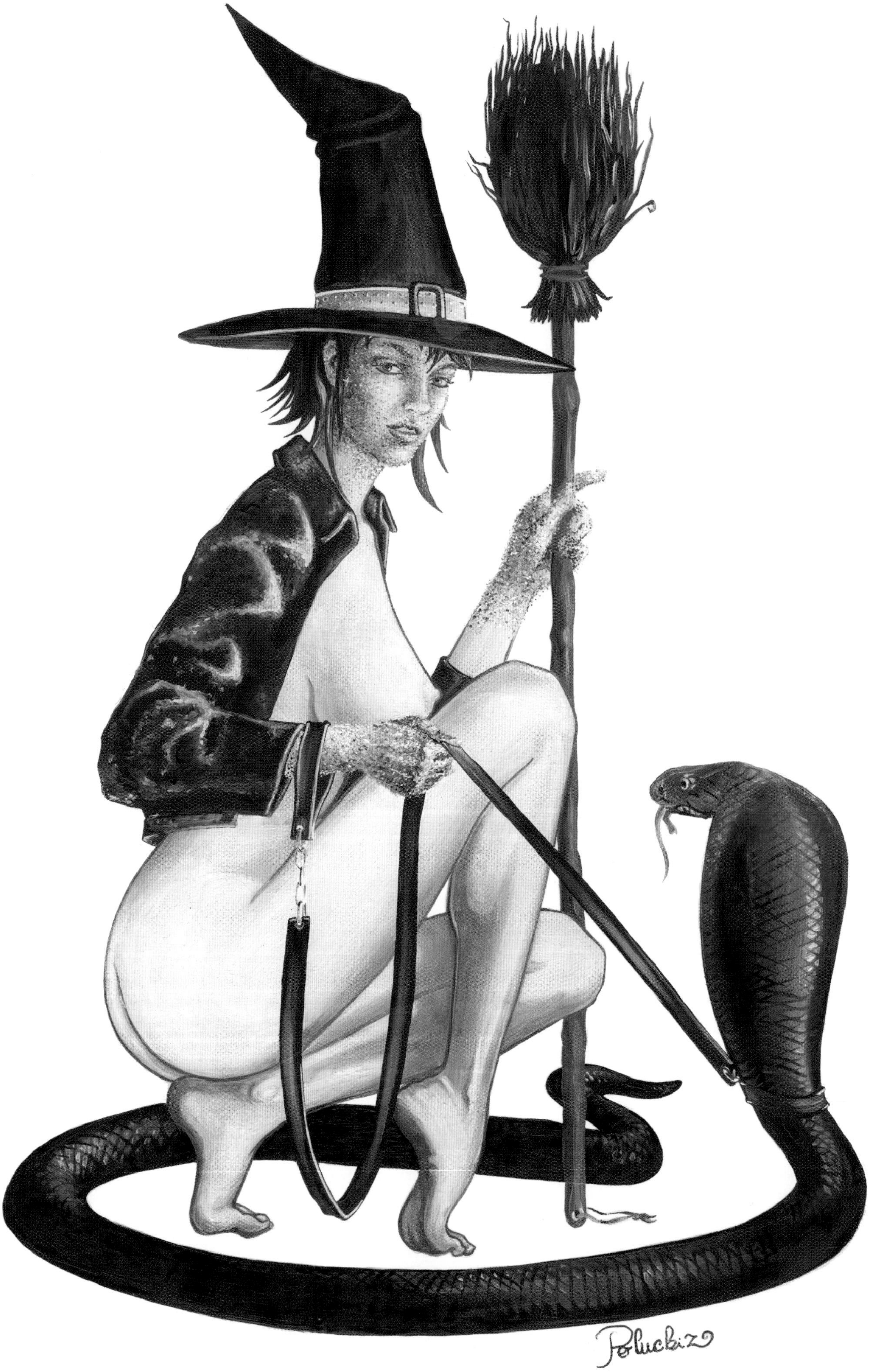
Perluckiz

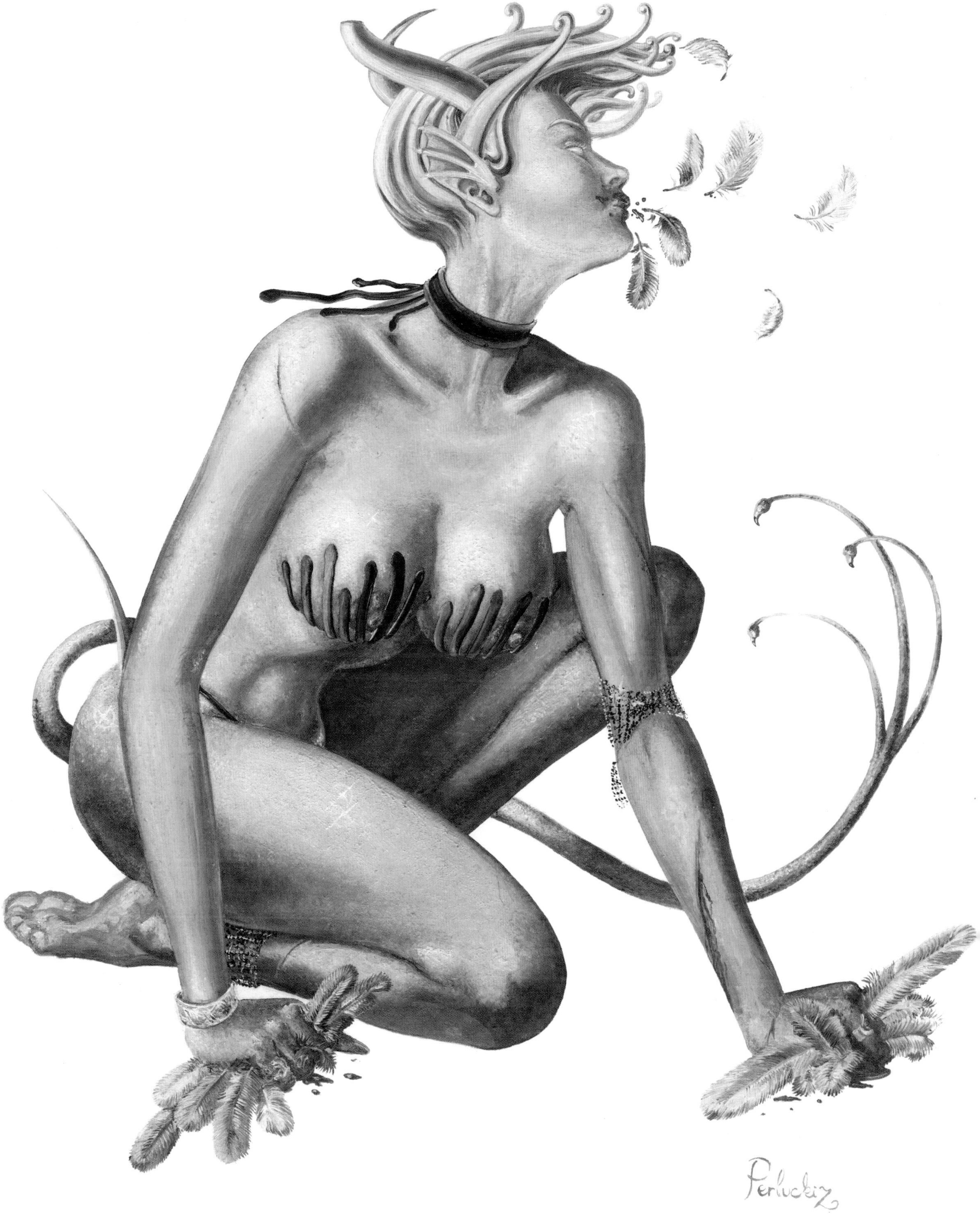
Perluckiz

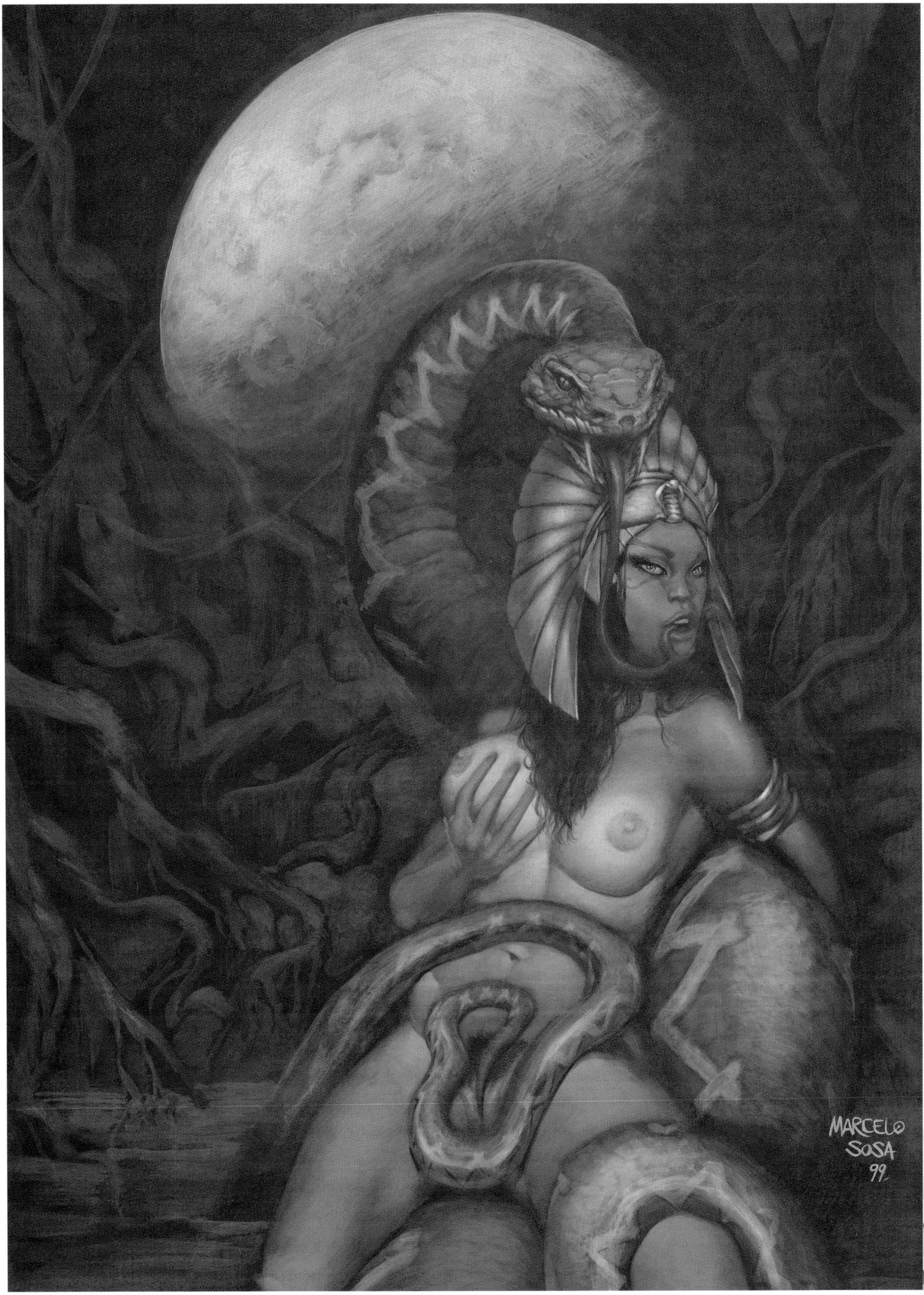
MARCELO
SOSA
99

Artwork by Marcelo Sosa

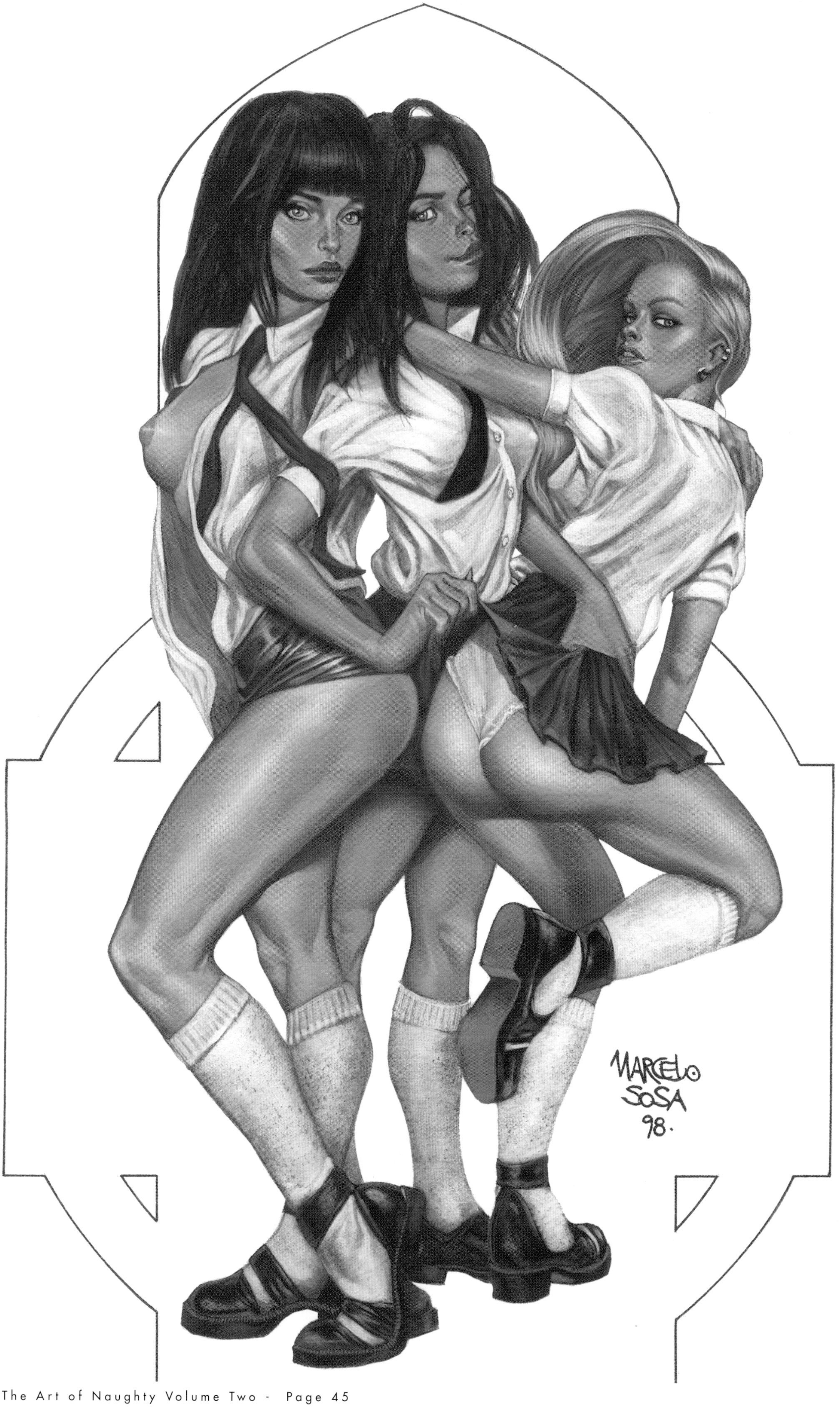
MARCELO
SOSA
98.

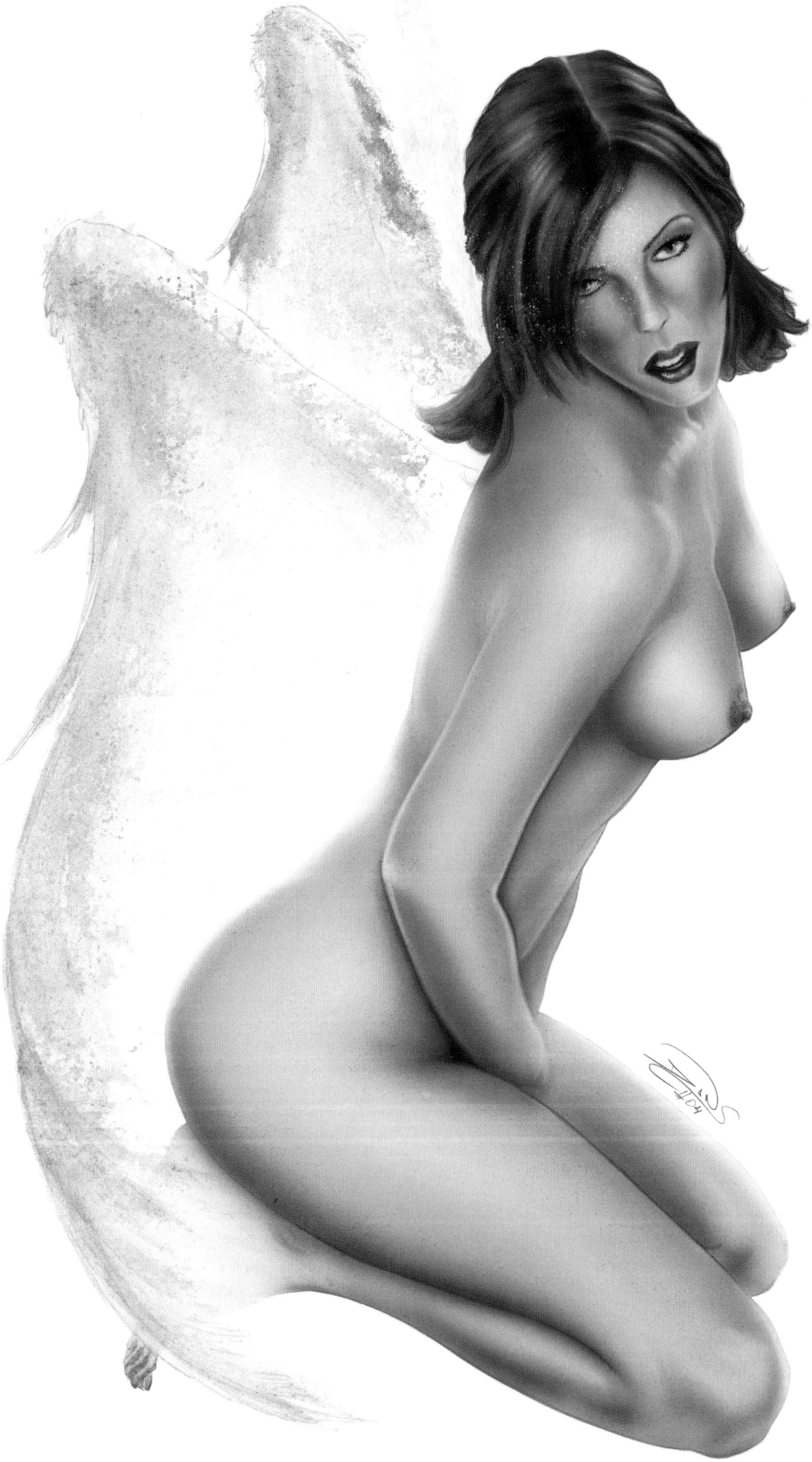

Artwork by Daniel Suarez

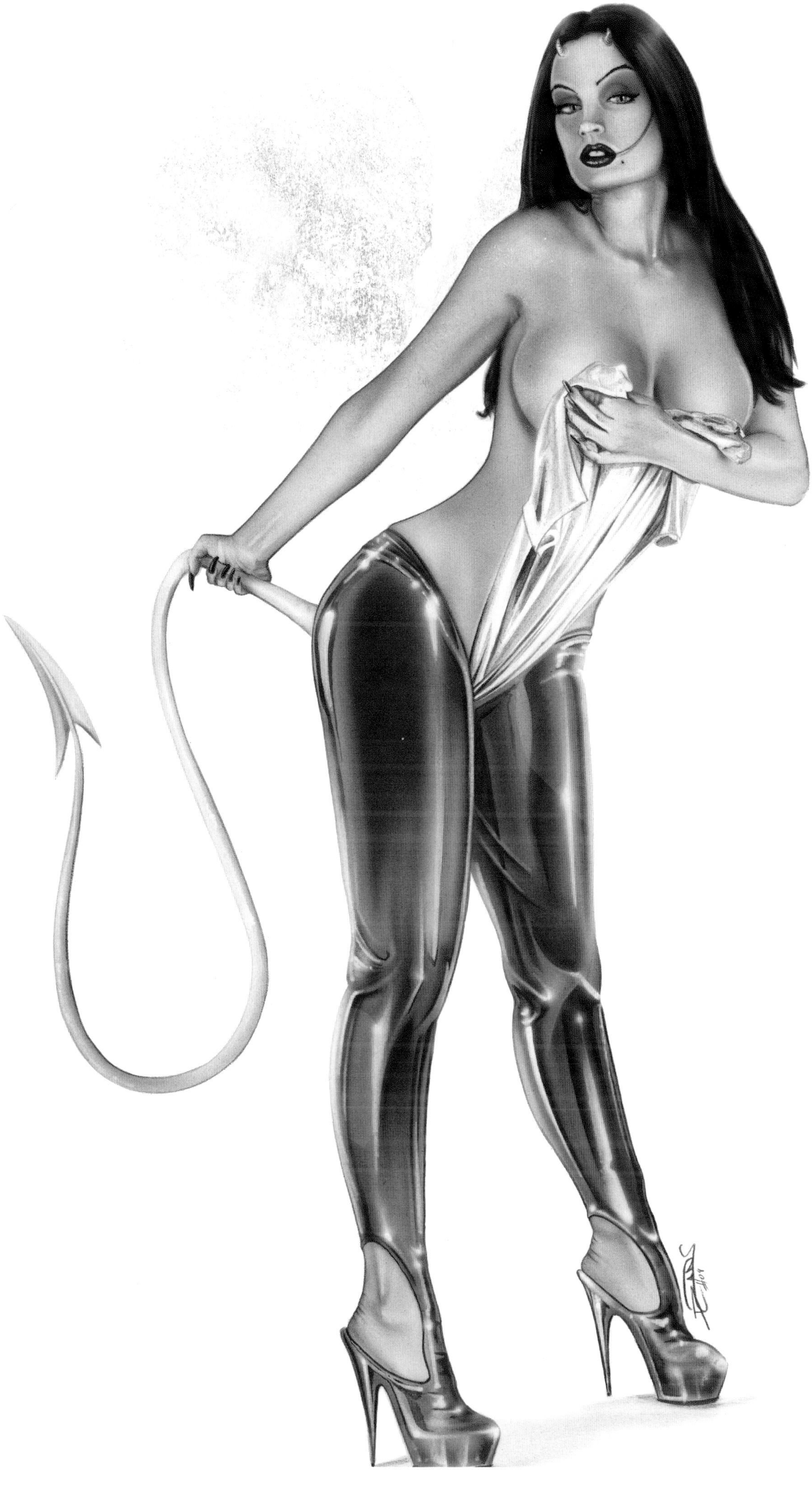